THE WORLD'S CLASSIC AIRCRAFT

THE WORLD'S CLASSIC AIRCRAFT

MIKE JERRAM

Galahad Books · New York City

AUTHOR'S ACKNOWLEDGMENTS

First published in the United
States of America in 1981 by
Galahad Books
95 Madison Avenue
New York, New York 10016
By arrangement with
Charles Herridge Ltd
Tower House, Abbotsham,
Devon, England

Library of Congress Catalog
Card Number: 80-85446

ISBN: 0-88365-554-3

Printed in Italy

Many people have contributed to the writing of this book, unselfishly sharing their knowledge, experience and their cockpits with me over a number of years. Special thanks are due to the following: David C. Frailey of American Airlines; Frank Pedroja of Beech Aircraft Corp.; Gordon Williams of Boeing Commercial Airplane Co.; John Farley and G. Lillistone of British Aerospace Kingston-Brough Division; Malcolm Ginsberg of CSE Aviation, Oxford; Stuart McKay of the D.H. Moth Club; Julie Gersuk of Ford Motor Co.; Rob Mack of General Dynamics Corp., Fort Worth; G. Donald Adams of Greenfield Village and Henry Ford Museum, Dearborn, Michigan; Geoffrey Norris and Mrs. Karen Stubberfield of McDonnell-Douglas Europe; Herr Polster of Messerschmitt-Bölkow-Blohm; Philip Edwards of the National Air & Space Museum, Washington D.C.; James Gilbert, Editor of *Pilot* Magazine; Stephen Piercey, Editor of *Propliner* Magazine; Gene Boswell of Rockwell International North American Division; Cole Palen and the late Dave Fox of Old Rhinebeck Aerodrome, New York State; Jack Bruce ISO, MA, FRHistS, MRAeS of the Royal Air Force Museum, Hendon; David Ogilvy of the Shuttleworth Trust; Lieutenant Toivo H. Nei of the United States Air Force 20th Tactical Fighter Wing, RAF Upper Heyford; Robert Carlisle of the United States Navy's Department of Photojournalism; Mike Beach; the late Captain Charles Blair; Austin J. Brown; the late Don Bullock; Captain Alan Chalkley; David Davies; Jeremy Flack; Brian Gates; Professor C.H. Gibbs-Smith, MA, FMA, Hon CRAeS; Captain Ron Gillies; Mike Hooks; Philip Jarrett; the late Manx Kelly; Curtis Pitts; Wim Schoenmaker; Mike Vines; the late Neil Williams; Philip Wolf; and the public relations staffs of: Air France; Alia Royal Jordanian Airline; British Aerospace; British Airways; Cessna Aircraft Company; Gates-Learjet Corporation; Piper Aircraft Corporation; Rolls-Royce (1971) Limited; Shorts, Belfast; United Airlines; and Vickers Limited.

Mike Jerram,
Southsea, Hampshire, England
March 1981

CONTENTS

Wright Flyer

This biplane is the shape of human flight.
Its name might better be first motor kite.
Its maker's name, time cannot get that wrong,
For it was writ in Heaven, doubly — Wright.

Thus poet Robert Frost paid tribute to what is perhaps the most famous aeroplane of all time — the Wright brothers' Flyer. Unless you give credence to the Russians' belated claim, not made until 1949, that their man Alexander Feodorovich Mozhaiski beat the Wrights to it by two decades, the Flyer made man's first ever controlled powered flight from the sand dunes at Kitty Hawk, North Carolina on 17 December 1903.

It was the culmination of several years' experimentation by the two Dayton, Ohio, bicycle makers, Wilbur and Orville Wright. Wilbur had been infatuated with the notion of mechanical flight since boyhood. In 1899 he confided to Professor Samuel P. Langley, director of the Smithsonian Institution in Washington, D.C., that he was convinced that human flight was at least possible and that he was about to embark on a thorough and systematic study of the subject prior to some practical experiments. 'I am an enthusiast, but not a crank,' he assured him.

During the years that followed, the two Wrights pursued their scientific study of flight with zeal. They built a wind-tunnel to evaluate wing airfoil sections, using the knowledge gained to construct a series of biplane gliders which were flown both as tethered kites and in free controlled glides from Big Kill Devil Hill, Kitty Hawk, in the summers of 1902 and 1903.

Few of the Wrights' predecessors or contemporaries had appreciated the need for aerodynamic control, assuming that their machines would have natural stability. Orville and Wilbur had no such delusion. Early in their trials they introduced wing-warping for lateral control of their gliders, providing a measure of roll control by means of a rocking cradle arrangement on which the pilot lay atop the wing. The prone piloting position was chosen to lessen wind resistance.

In a 39-day period of flight testing in the autumn of 1902 the brothers made nearly one thousand glides, employing wing-warping, a forward-mounted 'rudder' (which we would now refer to as a canard or forward elevator), and a vertical stabilizer at the rear to counter their machines' tendency to 'sidle' into the ground in a turn. They had thus achieved control in all three axes — roll, pitch and yaw, though their intention in providing the controls was at this stage more to prevent the gliders going their own way then to make them go where the Wrights wanted.

There remained the problem of motive power. Gliding, even controlled gliding, was not new, but a lightweight source of power for sustained flight had long eluded experimenters. After running tests to determine the optimum power/weight ratio for their machine, the Wrights designed and built their own engine. It was a watercooled in-line four-cylinder motor with an aluminium block. It was crude, heavy at 200 lbs with water, oil and one gallon of petrol, and though it peaked briefly at about 16 hp at 1,200 rpm, overheating quickly reduced its output to nearer 12 hp, which was barely sufficient for their purpose. With little previous research available to them, the Wrights designed their own propellers, quickly realizing that the popular assumption that a propeller screwed its way through the air was wrong. What was needed was in effect a rotating wing surface, so they made their eight-foot diameter blades of airfoil section and thus achieved a remarkable 66 per cent

efficiency in converting torque to thrust. The pusher propellers were linked to the engine by a pair of chains (they were not, as popular myth would have us believe, bicycle chains), one of which was crossed so that the two propellers counter-rotated, eliminating torque effect, and the engine itself was offset to the right, to counter-balance the weight of the pilot, who lay along the aircraft's centreline, and to ensure that it did not crush him in the event of an accident. The right wing panel was made four inches longer than the left to compensate for the weight differential between pilot and engine.

The biplane's wing warping was controlled by the movement of the pilot's hips in the cradle upon which he lay, and which was also connected to the rear rudder to co-ordinate turns. The forward elevator was controlled by rotating a horizontal winding-shaft with both hands. There was no provision for engine control save for a pull-string fuel cut-off. For 'launching' the Flyer the Wrights devised a trolley made up from adapted bicycle wheel hubs which ran on a 60-foot long wooden monorail track. The Flyer rested on top of the trolley, held back by a rope attached to the monorail which the pilot slipped when ready to take-off.

The first attempt, on Monday 14 December 1903, ended in failure. 'We tossed up a coin to decide who should make the first trial, and Will won,' Orville noted in his diary. 'While I was signalling the man

Perhaps the most famous photograph in aviation history, the Wright brothers' first successful powered flight at Kitty Hawk, 17 December 1903, snapped by John T. Daniels as the Flyer left the launching rail.

The Wright 1908 Military Aeroplane making a flight of one hour two and a quarter minutes at Fort Myer, Virginia, on 9 September 1908.

A closer view showing the chain drive to the propellers.

at the other end to leave go, and before I myself was ready, Will started the machine. I grabbed the upright the best I could and off we went. By the time we had reached the last quarter of the third rail the speed was so great I could stay with it no longer. I snapped my watch as the machine passed the end of the track [it had risen perhaps six or eight feet from the track's end]. The machine turned up in front and rose to a height of about 15 feet . . . [but] after losing most of its headway it gradually sank to the ground, turned up at an angle of probably 20 degrees incidence.'

The Flyer slewed into the sand, breaking a skid and some struts, but without injury to Wilbur. The incident described by Orville illustrates a feature of the Flyer which the brothers had stumbled upon unknowingly and which undoubtedly had saved their lives during their many gliding flights. By choosing their 'forward rudder' or elevator instead of opting for a rear-mounted surface they had unwittingly provided an anti-stall device, so that when the aircraft approached the stall (as it had in Orville's description above), it did not pitch down violently or enter a spin, but parachuted down in a flat, nose-high attitude.

Three days later Orville made the historic first controlled flight. It lasted only 12 seconds, but the brothers took it in turns to make three more flights, culminating in a 59-second, 852-foot trip across the sands. The original Flyer never flew again, which is perhaps as well for it was woefully unstable in pitch, flying in a series of phugoidal swoops, first rearing

up, then darting for the ground. That forward elevator was to blame. It was mounted too close to the wing to provide manageable pitch control, and its pivot-point, set exactly at mid-chord, made it much too sensitive. An elevator hinged at its forward edge tends naturally to trail in a neutral position when no control input is being made. Pitch stability was to be a problem with Wright biplanes for some time. Recent computer simulations of the Flyer's control system suggest that a *fixed* forward elevator would have given the machine 'hands-off' stability. The forward elevator did give the Wrights one big advantage though, for it provided a visual reference of the aeroplane's pitch attitude against the horizon. Few other pilots sitting out in the open in the pioneering days of flight had that.

Back home in Ohio in 1904 the Wrights prepared another Flyer, but were disappointed with their first attempts in what had promised to be an exciting season. The machine resisted all attempts to make it fly. Wilbur thought they might be 'a little rusty'. Historian Harry Combs has advanced another theory in his book *Kill Devil Hill*. The problem, says Combs, was simply density altitude — the relationship between air temperature and pressure which at low altitude and in cool conditions provides good 'thick' air to sustain an aeroplane in flight, but which at high altitude and temperatures (colloquially known as 'hot and high' among pilots) is thin and unsupportive. Hence the references among early fliers to days when 'there was no lift in the air'. At Kitty Hawk, which was at sea level, the December temperature had been 34 degrees Fahrenheit, producing an effective density altitude of 1,800 feet *below* sea level. At Huffman Prairie in Ohio, 815 feet above sea level, the springtime temperature was 81 degrees Fahrenheit, equating to a density altitude of 2,900 feet above sea level — a difference of 4,700 feet. The density altitude also served to rob the Wrights' engine of power which it could ill-afford to lose, as the rarified atmosphere of high altitudes will with any air-breathing powerplant. The brothers devised a weight-and-pulley-operated catapult to launch the Flyer and were soon making wide circling flights which, in the words of one observer, were 'one of the grandest sights of my life'. By the end of 1905 they were making flights up to 39 minutes duration and felt ready to offer their wonderful machine to an eager market. Alas, the market was neither eager nor ready. Faced with disinterest from the US Government and scepticism from the public, the brothers did not fly again for two and a half years. When they returned to Kitty Hawk in the spring of 1908 they had in their pockets a contract for a demonstration tour of France, and were bidding for a US War Department order for an aeroplane which would carry two people at 40 mph for ten miles — modest enough requirements, but in those days seemingly as likely as a journey to the moon.

The 1908 Flyer had a 30 hp engine. The pilot now sat upright, instead of lying on the hip-cradle, and — wonder of wonders — there was a passenger seat! The hip-cradle control system was replaced by two

newspaper called the Wrights 'bluffers'. But after his first public flight, which lasted but two minutes, a veteran French pioneer threw up his arms in surrender. *'Eh bien,'* he exclaimed, 'We are beaten. We do not exist!' Wilbur Wright made over one hundred flights in France, including one which lasted two hours, twenty minutes, twenty-three seconds. He carried innumerable passengers. One, Major Baden-Powell, brother of the founder of the Boy Scout movement, noted that 'the Flyer, while acting so satisfactorily, so perfectly, was yet very crude and even clumsy as regards many of its fittings and appendages'.

Giving the lie to the old adage that aeroplanes would frighten horses (attributed to an apoplectic old cavalryman when it was suggested that flying machines might have military applications), Wilbur Wright soars with a passenger over some untroubled horses at Pau, France, in 1909.

levers. On the right was the pitch lever, which operated in the natural sense: *forwards* to pitch the nose down away from the pilot, *back* to pitch it up towards him. On the left, between the seats, a second lever controlled roll: *forwards* to roll left, *backwards* for a right turn. The Wrights constantly altered their control systems, employing nine different methods in all. Often they would rig different systems on successive flights. It is a credit to their skills that they were able to explore and develop the basics of airmanship while contending with varying operating methods which required them virtually to relearn the handling of their machines each time they flew.

When Wilbur flew at Le Mans at the start of his 1908 tour, Europeans, whose own progress in aviation had thus far been dismal, were unbelieving. Paris

Crude perhaps, but it flew, and Europeans were dazzled by Wilbur's self-evident mastery of his element. Most extraordinary of all was how two obscure bicycle mechanics discovered in just four short years the secret which had for so long been denied the world's greatest inventors. In truth the Wright brothers were not the simple country boys of popular supposition. Their approach to the problem of powered flight was nothing if not scientific, and their achievement owed little to the work of their forerunners, save perhaps for inspiration. By our standards the 1903 Wright Flyer was an appalling flying machine which no modern pilot would surely be able to fly at all. And that is perhaps the greatest tribute one could pay to the determination and skills of Bishop Wright's two boys.

Blériot Monoplane

Many a bizarre mode of transport has been used to bridge the narrow stretch of water which separates England from France at their closest points: hang-gliders, kites, parachutes, an amphibious car, a buoyant bicycle, even a bathtub. Swimmers coated in thick lashings of grease frequently attempt the 21-mile journey. But never was there such a portentous voyage between those two

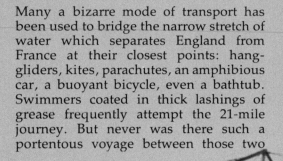

nations as that of Louis Blériot on 25 July 1909. Not since 1066 had a Frenchman's arrival on English soil been of such epoch-making significance to the insular British, whose leading newspaper *The Times* had once combined chauvinism with the Englishman's obsession with the weather in a splendid headline: *Fog in Channel: Continent cut off.* 'Britain is no longer an island!' the press baron Lord Northcliffe warned as he handed over a £1,000 prize to Blériot, whose aeroplane had flopped exhausted near Dover Castle after a 37-minute flight from Sangatte on the French coast.

The prize had not been Blériot's goal. Nor was his aeroplane, so charmingly referred to by the Dover Customs man who inspected it for contraband or contagious disease as a 'vessel', his first effort: the crutches made necessary by the failure of a previous machine were strapped to the fuselage side of his monoplane.

Blériot had made his fortune in the manufacture of acetylene lamps for motor cars, and frittered much of it away on a series of flying machines. No sooner would he wreck one than he would commence work on another, as likely as not one of an entirely different configuration. At one time he was attempting to fly three machines, but he settled at length on the now-conventional tractor monoplane configuration, with engine and wings at the front and the stabilizing tail surfaces at the rear. Blériot's cross-Channel attempt in his eleventh design was an attempt to publicize his machine, and it succeeded handsomely, Two days after

This 1909 Blériot XI was formerly used by the Blériot School at Hendon Aerodrome until 1912 and is now part of the Shuttleworth Collection at Old Warden Aerodrome, Bedfordshire, England, where it is the oldest airworthy aircraft in the Collection and probably in the world.

Elaborate undercarriage geometry of the Blériot XI can be seen in this view of an example preserved at the Royal Air Force Museum, Hendon. The engine is a Gnôme rotary which substantially improved the aircraft's performance over that achieved with the three-cylinder Anzani.

his landfall at Dover, Monsieur Blériot had received orders for 100 of his monoplanes. Within two years there were three times more Blériot types flying in Europe than all other makes combined, and the Type XI was the mainstay of pilot training schools and embryonic air forces throughout the world.

In many respects the Blériot XI was a very 'modern' aeroplane for 1909. Tiny,

with a wingspan of just 25 feet, it had broad, heavily-cambered wings braced by wires which fanned out from a central kingpost like a Maypole. A flexible mainspar and lightweight structure enabled the outer portions of the wings to be warped for lateral control, using the technique perfected by the Wright brothers but in 1909 still not widely adopted in Europe. Blériot had himself made early experiments with hinged ailerons, but abandoned them. The cross-Channel Blériot was the first aeroplane to employ a single control stick for pitch and roll commands, combined with a swivelling foot-bar to work its rudder. Control wires from the wings and the outer portions of the tailplane, which rotated on a tubular spar to act as elevators, were connected to the universally jointed stick by pulleys and support pylons, and by a patented bell housing known as a *cloche* at the base of the stick, which had a fixed wheel handgrip at the top. The stick worked in the logical sense: left or right to dip the appropriate wing, forward to lower the nose, back to raise it.

The fuselage was an open, truss-rigged wooden frame with snap-on canvas covers to protect the pilot in his basket-weave seat. The engine of the cross-Channel machine was a three-cylinder aircooled 25 hp Anzani, the product of an Italian motorcycle racer and engine wizard named Alessandro Anzani, who was noted for his appallingly bad language. It is not surprising that he was given to cursing, for his engines were not the most co-operative powerplants, being rather prone to overheating and thus losing what meagre power they had to start with, as Blériot discovered. His Anzani, probably having the longest uninterrupted run of its life, started to overheat badly in mid-Channel, and he looked set for a ducking when a rain-shower cooled the motor's cylinders (and Blériot's temper) and kept the Anzani running long enough to reach Dover's cliffs. Later Blériots were powered by Gnome rotary engines which were much more reliable — with luck they might run for anything up to 12 hours without over-haul — and gave the Monoplane a sprightly performance.

Back in Edwardian times a young gentleman seeking to learn the art of aviating would likely have had an Anzani-engined Blériot as his tutor. Before taking to the air he would first be let loose on a *Penguin* — an old Blériot whose wings had been clipped short so that, like its namesake, it was incapable of flight but could make tentative hops, bounding across the grass at the Blériot School's base at Hendon Aerodrome, or at Buc, near Paris, while the apprentice airman accustomed himself to the feel of its controls and to the Blériot's tricky ground handling.

A Blériot on the ground was never easy to control because its bicycle-wheeled undercarriage, sprung with rubber bungee cord, was free-castoring

and had its own ideas of where to go. At low speeds the tiny rudder was of little help in controlling direction, so an inexperienced pilot would inevitably go skating and tail-chasing across the flying field on his first attempts at riding a *Penguin*. Even getting aboard a Blériot could be difficult, because as you took hold of the fuselage sides to mount the cockpit the aeroplane would sidle away on its castoring wheels, like a horse shying from a strange rider.

Having tamed his *Penguin*, our fledgling aviator would graduate to the real thing, encouraged perhaps by the knowledge that Louis Blériot had had less than five hours total flying experience when he made his cross-Channel flight. There were few instruments to worry over on an Anzani Blériot, not even a tachometer. He checked the health of his Anzani with an eye on the throbbing oil pulsometer glass. *Contact!* A mechanic would swing the six foot ten inch diameter scimitar-bladed propeller, and if the Anzani was feeling benevolent it would burst into a popcorn machine caco-phony — *pok-pok-pok-pok-a-tapoketa-pok-pok*. The pilot would turn swiftly into wind and begin the take-off run, vision blurred like an out-of-focus snapshot by the engine's vibration. An Anzani which was 'on song' would produce 25 hp at about 1,400 rpm (there was no throttle,

A polished wood steering wheel topped off Blériot's patented control column, the first to combine pitch and roll commands in a single control. The leather strap is to prevent prying hands moving the controls of this museum-preserved Blériot XI.

French pilot M. Salmet passing over Scarborough beach during a *Daily Mail*-sponsored tour of English coastal resorts. Note the passenger waving from the rear seat of the Blériot XI.

just an ignition advance/retard lever on the control wheel), but flying school Blériots' Anzanis were usually singing off key and would put out about 22 hp at best. The single-stick/footbar controls made the Blériot easier to handle than many of its contemporaries, but the warping wings and tiny rudder gave poor control response at the low airspeed (25-35 mph) at which they mostly flew. The elevators were powerfully effective and sensitive. A moment's inattention would cause the nose of the machine to rear up, for the Anzani-engined Blériots were tail-heavy and needed a slight nose-down stick force to maintain level flight with power. This was of course before the days of control surface trimming whereby stick loads could be trimmed out either by means of aerodynamic tabs attached to the surface or by tensioning control cables to maintain a desired attitude. An Anzani Blériot pilot had only to sneeze or let his attention wander and the nose would come up, the airspeed would fall very quickly, and a stall would ensure shortly after, for these early aeroplanes flew precariously close to the stall at all times. So twitchy was the Blériot that even an inch of forward or backward movement on the stick would produce a substantial pitch change.

With double the power of an Anzani the Gnome-engined Blériots were fine performers, much exploited by the earliest pioneers of aerobatics. Celestin Adolphe Pégoud, who so impressed Louis Blériot as a student at his school at Buc that he hired him as a test pilot, flew a specially-strengthened Type XI in which he first performed a vertical-S manoeuvre in September 1913. Later that month he looped-the-loop for the first time in public, made steep sideslips, tailslides, spiral dives, and manoeuvres reported as 'capsizes' and 'side-somersaults'. It is unlikely that the Blériot's poor lateral control would have made a rolling manoeuvre possible: probably Pégoud succeeded in banking his machine to the vertical position and then recovered erect. Pégoud later repeated these remarkable aerobatics for a sceptical British public at Brooklands Aerodrome near London, and was that evening feted at a celebration dinner given by the great English pioneering airman Claude Grahame-White at the Royal Automobile Club. Tables were laid inverted, menus printed backwards and the meal served in reverse order, commencing with coffee and finishing with the hors d'oeuvre, while a caberet was performed by artistes standing on their heads! Pégoud was probably the most comfortable man present. Before attempting his aerial antics he had spent hours strapped into the cockpit of his machine inverted in a hangar, to accustom himself to the sensation of upside-down flight. Many young blades began 'Pégoud-ing', resulting in a French War Ministry ban on stunting following a rash of fatal attempts to copy his act.

For an average student flier, just getting his Blériot back on the ground was enough. 'Volplaning', or making a power-off glide approach, was a risky procedure in a Blériot, or indeed in any of the early flying machines, which had high drag characteristics and glided steeply at angles of about 30 degrees. Few novices attempted to glide-land. The Blériot's bungee-spring landing gear did take some of the shock out of hard arrivals and the natural tail-sitting stance of the Anzani-engined machines helped attain the three-point attitude which was essential at touchdown to avoid a precarious ride on the castoring mainwheels.

Although it is best remembered for that 1909 flight from France to England, the Blériot Monoplane had much greater significance. It was the first truly practical monoplane, whose design was to influence the development of aeroplances for decades, and it was one of the first machines to be mass-produced, filling those orders which were showered on Louis Blériot in the euphoria following his flight.

The Shuttleworth Trust's Anzani-engined Blériot XI taking off from Old Warden Aerodrome.

Avro 504

Table napkins and the backs of old envelopes gave birth to many an aeroplane in the days when new designs were the products of a single creative mind, a scrap of paper and stub of pencil. Alliot Verdon-Roe favoured penny notebooks, and it was on such modest stationery that he roughed out the first sketches of his most enduring design, and one of the world's most successful aircraft — the Avro 504.

Roe, the son of a Manchester doctor, tried aviation after dabbling in fishing, tree-planting, surveying, running a post-office, railroading and marine engineering. While serving aboard ship he became fascinated by the albatrosses which wheeled above him, and on his return home he started experimenting with paper gliders which he would launch from the top floor of his parents' house, to the amusement of inmates of the lunatic asylum next door who thought he was another of their kind. On 8 June 1908, Roe succeeded in making a 150-foot hop in a full-size biplane design, completing the first ever powered flight by an Englishman, though his achievement never gained official recognition.

In the spring of 1913 Roe, now well established as an aircraft designer and manufacturer, roughed out a series of pencil sketches for a new biplane. Roughed-out is perhaps the wrong term, for those surviving penny-notebook drawings reveal a high standard of draughtsmanship and a close attention to the detail of even the smallest fittings for

This side elevation of the prototype Avro 504 shows well the 'toothpick' undercarriage skid designed to prevent the aircraft nosing over on the ground, and the distinctive 'comma' rudder.

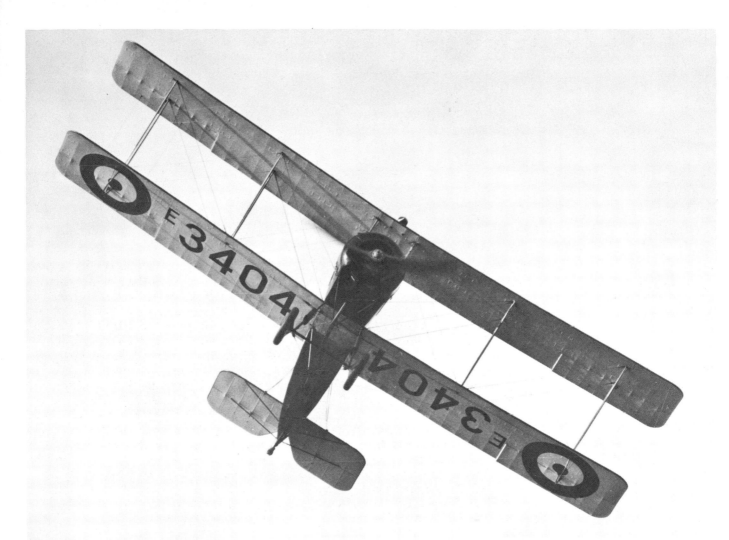

the new Avro Type 504. It was to be a two-seat, tandem, open-cockpit machine with heavily staggered wings for improved downward and forward vision, a streamline-cowled Gnome rotary engine and a characteristic Roe under-carriage incorporating a central 'toothpick' skid between the rubber-sprung, telescopic, mainwheel legs.

In his 504, Roe created a design which was instinctively right from the outset. Early flight trials at Brooklands race track in the hands of test pilot Fred Raynham revealed superlative handling, though the original wing-warping was soon replaced by hinged ailerons for roll control. The airframe was a masterly piece of engineering, though one onlooker remarked to Roe that it seemed astonishingly light. 'It should rather be said that it is astonishingly strong for its weight,' admonished Roe, pointing out that the Avro company worked to Admiralty stress requirements, not to the more lenient demands of the War Office.

Roe thought he might win orders for six aircraft. As things turned out, it was a slightly pessimistic prediction. By

Armistice Day 1918, 8,340 Avro 504s had been built. When production finally ended in 1933 the total had risen to more than 10,000, and few indeed were the British pilots who had not logged some time in a 504, for tens of thousands of trainees took their first faltering flights in Avros.

Most numerous of the many 504 types was the 504K, powered by a 100 hp Gnome Monosoupape rotary engine (and less commonly by 100 hp Le Rhône or 130 hp Clerget powerplants, all of which fitted a standard engine mount). This was the archetypal training machine, developed from earlier fighter-bomber Avro 504As and 'Bs (despite Roe's adherence to doing things the Admiralty way, they insisted on structural improvements to their Avros before placing an order, hence the Royal Flying Corps A and Royal Naval Air Service B variants) which achieved the double distinction of being the first Allied aircraft shot down during World War 1 and the first to bomb Germany.

As a raw recruit to the Royal Flying Corps or Royal Naval Air Service you

The Shuttleworth Trust's Avro 504K (actually a later model 504N converted back to World War I standard) is the only example flying in Britain.

would study your copy of the official *Pilot's Notes* and be comforted to learn that 'running the engine is simple'. Hah! So young, so gullible. You would soon learn that handling the cantankerous Gnome was the most difficult part of your training. As its name implied, the Gnome Monosoupape had but a single valve in each of its seven cylinders, serving as both exhaust and air inlet valve. Engine control was achieved by a lever which moved a tapered needle in a regulating valve for mixture control. There was no carburettor and no throttle, just an on-off 'blip' switch. The 'Mono' responded well enough to a sensitive hand, but the two-thumbed fumblings of a tyro would

often result in a sudden and embarrassing loss of power through over-rich mixture just when you least needed it, or an equally sudden and unwanted burst of energy.

Starting up followed the familiar rotary ritual: pump up fuel pressure to the regulating valve to three-and-a-half pounds per square inch (a relief valve blew off at four pounds if you overdid it), push petrol lever fully *open*, magneto switch *off* for sucking in fuel/air mixture, then petrol *off*, magneto switch *on* as the mechanic 'armstronged' the propeller. 'If the engine fires put petrol about one inch on adjustment,' advised the *Notes,* 'and with the stick well back buzz the engine

slowly until the oil begins to pulsate in the pulsator glass, then increase the amount of petrol until the sound of the engine is crisp and regular.' You may occasionally hear reference to 'rattling, vibrating rotary engines.' Not so. Well-balanced rotaries ran sewing-machine smooth, tranquil as turbines, with far less vibration than modern four-cylinder horizontally-opposed powerplants.

'Ready then?', your instructor in the rear cockpit would call through the Gosport Tube. This device, named after the School of Special Flying established at Gosport on England's south coast by the father of modern flight training, Major Robert Smith-Barry, was little more than

an aerial adaptation of the speaking tube. In the earliest days of flying instruction, inter-cockpit communication took the form of thought transmission through a quick waggle of the control stick or a scribbled note thrust out against the slipstream. Gosport Tubes were better than that, but only just.

Watch the swing to the left as you open up for take-off, and correct with a little right rudder. *Gently, gently!* The light, finless, balanced rudder is powerful. Careful not to overcorrect, or your tail will come round to meet your nose and we'll be walking all the way over to stores to indent for one new Avro, price £870 without the engine. Many a student

Delightful study of the Shuttleworth Trust's Avro 504K flying near its home base.

Another view of the Shuttleworth Avro 504K.

must have made that sheepish walk, for only about 3,000 of the 8,000 Avros built during the War were still on charge in November 1918.

In a good breeze the lightweight Avro would be airborne in twenty yards. A new one, clean and correctly rigged, would reach the practice area at 3,500 feet in five minutes and cruise at 70 mph, but more likely you would get a time-worn example with sloppy rigging and oil-soaked fabric which struggled gamely to manage 65 mph. Old-stagers like those were not popular. One Flying Training School officer allegedly developed a foolproof technique for 'accidentally'

crashing such machines with such skill that he could guarantee the resulting injury to the aircraft would exceed the Air Ministry's laid-down minimum of 50 per cent damage to justify replacement with a brand-new machine rather than make repairs . . .

The Avro was not difficult to fly by contemporary standards, but its controls were not especially well harmonized. The rudder was very sensitive, demanding delicate footwork, but the ailerons were sluggish and provoked adverse yaw (greater drag produced by the down going aileron tended to yaw the aircraft in the opposite direction to the turn) so that

There were two methods of starting an Avro: the 'Armstrong' method (hand-swinging), or by using a Hucks Starter which was based on a Model T Ford chassis and invented by the pioneer British aviator 'Benny' Hucks. The Hucks and Avro pictured here are owned by the Shuttleworth Trust Collection.

very precise rudder coordination was needed for balanced turns. Students were taught to feel for the balance of their turns by the breeze on their faces. Cold air on the cheek on the inside of the turn meant a sideslip. More rudder needed. A draught on the cheek to the outside of the turn signalled a skid, to be corrected by increasing bank and decreasing rudder deflection. In a correctly-balanced turn no draught should have been felt. It was this reliance upon wind-in-the-face flying that convinced pilots and aircraft designers for years that a machine with a fully-enclosed cockpit would be impossible to fly accurately.

Aerobatics in an Avro were limited by those insensitive ailerons, so that manoeuvres in the rolling plane were ponderous if not impossible, though the useful rudder could be employed to effect a half-roll (you had to cling onto the underside of the seat when inverted because the 504 had only a simple lap-strap) or even a barrel roll. Loops were tight thanks to the aeroplane's low wing loading, and easily accomplished from a dive to 90 mph. You closed the petrol fine-adjustment lever over the top of the loop to prevent the Mono overspeeding in the vertical dive, and remembered to open it again as soon as level flight was regained or the engine would soon stop. The Avro was a fine machine for practising spins, which it would perform with enthusiasm and without warning if stalled carelessly, but it spun slowly, lost little altitude for every turn, and could easily be recovered. Such attributes made it a marvellous mount for performing the attractive but now rarely seen falling-leaf manoeuvre, in which the aircraft descends in a series of checked spins in alternate directions.

Ready for landing? Remember that the rubber bungee cord suspension will magnify your every bounce into a kangaroo hop across the field if you misjudge your touch-down, and the lack of a progressive throttle means that you cannot juggle the power to smooth things out. Petrol lever closed, relax the right rudder you have been holding to counter-act torque, hold a steady 55 mph on the glide, taking care to keep her pointing into wind, for she's light and ready to drift on the merest zephyr. At 50 feet advance the petrol about an inch but hold the 'blip' switch down, levelling off about one foot above the grass, then back g-e-n-t-l-y on the stick so she touches on wheels and tailskid in the classic three-point attitude. Right, we'll try that again. Fuel lever forward, the Mono, still spinning under inertia, roars back to life and she's off the ground again in a few feet. You had to remember to lean the mixture again once the engine was running smoothly because the Mono was notoriously prone to 'rich cuts' — it would quickly lose power if the mixture was too rich, trailing a plume of black smoke for all (except you) to see, and down you would go very quickly. A rich-cut on take-off was especially dangerous because the lightly-loaded high-drag airframe lost flying speed very swiftly and would stall and perhaps spin within seconds unless you pushed the nose down to maintain airspeed. The correct technique following a rich-cut was to pull back the petrol lever and wait for seven or eight seconds, which seemed like hours, for the engine to pick up again. It was not uncommon for a student pilot flying solo to exaggerate the problem in his anxiety by enriching the mixture, for fear that fuel starvation was the source of his woes, and then, having thus ensured the necessity of a forced landing, close the petrol lever so that the engine would unchoke itself and come back on full song just as he was about to touch-down. With the problem seemingly resolved once more he would climb away (without remembering to bring the petrol lever forward again) and the Mono would cut dead. *Running the engine is simple,* the book said.

For all that, the Avro trained generations of pilots over three decades, and like its American counterpart the Curtiss JN-4 Jenny, became a favourite mount of post-war barnstormers and stunt-flyers, demobbed servicemen knowing no skill but flying who snapped up war-surplus Avros for as little as £25 and brought aviation to fairgrounds, beaches and farmers' meadows at five-bob a flip. The great pioneer Sir Alan Cobham used Avros in his flying circus and estimated that he carried more than one million people on joyrides, many in old 504s modified to carry two or sometimes three passengers. This verse, penned in 1919, sums up the Avro's barnstorming days:

Stranded at Brighton and bored to monotony,
Sadly I roamed by the crowd-haunted shore;
Fed up with bathing and boating and botany,
Languidly humming the strains of 'Asthore';
Then, in the offing, descended an aeroplane,
Gaily the pilot came striding my way;
'Afternoon, Sir!', he exclaimed,
'Would you dare a plane Voyage today?'

In an Avro, who wouldn't?

Fokker DR.1 Triplane

Early spring 1917 at an airfield in France. Two men are in earnest conversation. One wears a thick overcoat buttoned to the neck and a peaked cap, the other the long leather flying coat and uniform of the German Imperial Air Service: Anthony Fokker the Flying Dutchman, self-made millionaire and brilliant young aircraft designer, and Rittmeister Baron Manfred von Richthofen, commander of Jagdstaffel 11. Fokker wants to know how the German pilots are faring? Is their equipment satisfactory? What sorts of aeroplane will they need next? Richthofen takes him aside and shows him Jasta 11's latest prize. It is a British Sopwith Triplane, a new type on the Western Front which has the German fliers worried, for it has an astonishing rate of climb and is highly manoeuvrable. Richthofen's men would like such a machine. No, they would like one even better.

Later that year the Flugzeugmeisterei invited representatives from all the German aircraft manufacturers to inspect a captured Sopwith Triplane and let it be known that fat contracts were waiting for triplane designs. A rash of Dreideckers followed — no fewer than 34 prototypes were submitted eventually, but even as his rivals examined the British machine that day, Tony Fokker's own triplane was being readied for flight at his Schwerin factory.

The Fokker V3 prototype was the creation of Fokker's chief designer Reinhold Platz. Though he had no formal training save as a welder, Platz was an accomplished aero engineer. To him the triplane configuration was an antiquated absurdity, but he was long resigned to the whims of his employer and set to work designing a trio of cantilever wings (hence the V designation for *verspannungslos:* cantilever) with strong box-section spars which he mated to the typical Fokker welded steel frame fuselage. The Fokker design was no carbon copy of the Sopwith. It was smaller and more compact, with not a bracing wire or interplane strut between its wings. Their absence bothered the government test pilots who flew the V3 prototype. They complained that the wings flexed alarmingly in flight, so Fokker had single I-shaped interplane struts installed on the second machine to damp out wing vibrations, and had the control surfaces balanced. During destructive testing the triplane wings withstood a load of 7.75g before they began to fail. Few contemporary aircraft could take such loads.

When Manfred von Richthofen first flew the triplane in July 1917 he reported enthusiastically to his squadron pilots that is was 'as manoeuvrable as the devil and climbed like a monkey'. Orders for 320 production Fokker Dr.1s (Dr for *Dreidecker:* three decks) were placed and Tony Fokker personally delivered the first aircraft to Richthofen's Geschwader in August. Production was in full swing in October 1917 when, on 28th of that month, Staffelführer Heinrich Gontermann, a 39-victory ace from Jasta 15, took off in his newly-delivered triplane for the first time to perform some aerobatics over his home aerodrome. As he pulled out of a steep dive witnesses saw pieces fly from the Fokker's wings and it crashed, fatally injuring Gontermann. Next day a pilot from Richthofen's Jasta 11 was killed landing his Dreidecker.

All Dr.1s were immediately grounded for inspection, and it was found that cap strips, plywood webs and ribs themselves were parting from the aeroplanes' wing spars. Poor workmanship, faulty glueing and moisture had gone unnoticed in the rush to complete the new machines. Fokker was ordered to replace all Dr.1 wings without delay — and

opposite
No original Fokker Dr.1 Triplane survives. This one is an authentic replica which forms part of a flying circus of Great War types operated by a British theme park company, and is finished in the colours of one of Manfred von Richthofen's aircraft.

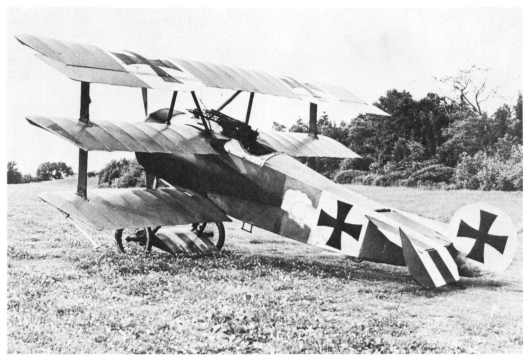

The single interplane struts joining the Fokker Dr.I's three wings were added after tests with a fully-cantilever prototype revealed wing flexing and vibration problems. The additional lifting surface over the wheel axles can be seen in this view of a Dreidecker replica in Cole Palen's collection at Old Rhinebeck Aerodrome, New York State.

without payment — meanwhile the machines were not to be flown.

It was a disaster so early in the life of a new aeroplane. Fokker and his workers soon made good the damage to the aeroplanes, and the ban was lifted within three weeks, but the damage done to the triplane's reputation was less easy to mend. Seeds of doubt had been sown in the minds of many pilots, and production of new airframes had been seriously delayed while existing machines were rebuilt. By May 1918, when the Dreidecker had been superseded in front-line service by the Mercedes-engined Fokker D.VII biplane, only 173 of the 320 aircraft ordered had been delivered, and the triplane's combat career was drawing to a premature close.

Why did Fokker opt for a triplane design? Power, or rather the lack of it. Fokker's Dutch nationality was resented by his German rivals. They saw to it that he was never able to obtain the latest watercooled Mercedes and BMW in-line engines for his aeroplanes. He had managed to acquire some 700 brand-new 110 hp Le Rhône rotary engines which had been licence-built in Sweden by the Thulin company, and these, each marked prominently with a plaque declaring it *Beute* (captured) for the sake of outwardly preserving Swedish neutrality, were earmarked for the Dr.1. Confined to old (though excellent) rotary engines, Fokker reasoned that if he could not go for speed, then rate of climb and manoeuvrability must be his aeroplane's forte. Even before Richthofen had shown him the captured

Sopwith, Fokker had settled on a triplane configuration to achieve his goal, and the Dr.1 bore out his judgement.

Such were the flying qualities of the triplane that its flexibility and manoeuvrability masked its weakness. Few Allied pilots who had combat encounters with the Fokker ever realized that it was quite appallingly slow, barely capable of 90 mph at 13,000 feet. But it could reach that altitude in 15 minutes and had an initial climb rate of 1,131 feet per minute. British and American test pilots who flew captured Dreideckers after war's end were astonished at its rate of climb and even more by its ability to make the sharpest turns without loss of altitude. By applying full rudder the triplane could be whipped round almost in its own length, reversing direction in a flat, skidding, unbanked turn. Only the Sopwith Camel came near to matching the Fokker's turning radius, and then only with a skilled campaigner at its controls.

The Dreidecker was not nearly so difficult to fly as the Camel. German pilots were sent off solo on the machine as soon as they had mastered a clip-winged Fokker E.1 Eindecker. Thanks to its low wing loading (there was a fourth lifting surface between the landing-gear legs providing a total wing area of 202 square feet for a gross weight of only 1,290 lbs) and thick airfoil section, the Dreidecker had excellent low-speed handling qualities, with a stall speed below 30 mph. But it was prone to ground-loop at the least provocation. Even a bump in the grass might start its tail coming

round, and the tiny comma-shaped rudder gave little help in keeping it straight during the landing roll.

The triplane's snappy handling made it a natural dogfighter. Ernst Udet called it his 'ideal fighting machine', and was so taken with his Dreidecker that he tried to have one specially built for him after the war as a personal sportsplane, foreshadowing by half a century a current passion for building Fokker Dr.1 replicas. More than 100 latter-day Dreideckers are flying, and they are the unchallenged favourites among World War I replica builders, which is fortunate because not a single original Dr.1 survives anywhere in the world. Manfred von Richthofen's blood red machine was destroyed in 1943 when the Royal Air Force bombed the Deutsches Museum in Berlin.

Despite its early failures and a drastically curtailed service career the Dreidecker is the aeroplane most frequently associated with the German air arm during the Great War. Why? Because of its link with two of Germany's leading aces: Werner Voss and Manfred von Richthofen, who immortalized the triplane and died in it.

Lieutenant Werner Voss of Jasta 10 was a former cavalryman who won the First Class Order of the Iron Cross when he was 18 years of age and then transferred to the Imperial Air Arm. Within a week of joining his first fighter squadron, the Flying Hussar had scored the first of his 49 victories. Voss went to war with considerable élan. Though frequently sloppy on the ground, he would don a fresh white silk shirt before flying on a patrol (allegedly so that he would be presentable for entertaining the ladies of Paris should he be shot down and captured), and commissioned an engraved silver cup for each of his victories. His silversmith must have been a busy man. After getting his Dr.1 (on whose cowling Voss painted a mustachioed face where the circular cooling holes for the engine formed natural 'eyes') he made ten confirmed kills in the space of three weeks, three of them in a single day. On the day of his last kill, 23 September 1917, Voss flew an evening patrol and was near Ypres when his flight of three Fokkers encountered a patrol of nine British S.E.5As from 56 Squadron Royal Flying Corps, led by Captains James McCudden and G.H. Bowman. After a brief skirmish Voss found himself surrounded by six British fighters. 'This did not appear to deter him in the slightest,' Bowman reported. 'He had a much better rate of climb or rather zoom than we, and frequently he was the highest machine of the six and could have turned east and got away if he had wished to, but he was not that type and always came down into us again. His machine was exceptionally manoeuvrable and he appeared to be taking flying liberties with impunity . . . I put my nose down to give him a burst and opened fire; to my amazement he kicked on full rudder without bank, pulled his nose up slightly, gave me a burst while he was skidding sideways, and then kicked on opposite rudder before the results of his amazing stunt appeared to have any

Anthony Fokker's Eindecker monoplanes decimated British scouts during the infamous Fokker Scourge of 1916. This is a replica of the E.III, typical of the Eindeckers with cat's cradle bracing wires and a single machine gun synchronized to fire through the revolving propeller.

effect on the controllability of his machine.' But as Voss's attention was distracted by his brush with Bowman, another RFC pilot, Lieutenant Rhys Davids, managed to get on his tail and emptied a whole drum of ammunition from his Lewis gun into the triplane. The Dreidecker continued its steady flight, seemingly gliding towards the British lines, where it crashed. Voss was dead. James McCudden later wrote of him: 'His flying was wonderful, his courage magnificent, and in my opinion he was the bravest German airman whom it has been my privilege to see fight,' while the victor, Rhys Davids, lamented into his celebration glass: 'Oh, if only I could have brought him down alive.'

Voss and his Dreidecker had been kindred spirits. So too was Manfred von Richthofen, a natural hunter whose combat rule was never to waste ammunition shooting holes in aeroplanes; always aim for the pilot or gunner and don't miss. Richthofen already had 59 victories when he flew a Dreidecker (in all he flew four different triplanes in an eight-month period) in combat for the first time on 2 September 1917, bringing down an RFC R.E.8 observation aircraft. Richthofen was a skilled, efficient and ruthless craftsman for whom the nimble Dreidecker was a natural extension of himself,

above
More than 100 Fokker Triplane replicas are flying. This one is an American-owned example built from the plans of homebuilder Ron Sands.

right
Cutaway of the Fokker Dr.I reveals typical Fokker welded steel tube fuselage and tail surfaces with wooden wings.

falling as easily to hand as a favourite shotgun might have. He rigged the control stick of his triplane with twin triggers for the Hispano machine guns so that he could fly and fire with the same hand, and thus equipped the Fokker was a formidable gun platform. Richthofen brought his total score up to 80 aircraft while flying triplanes (though two of those victories were made in an Albatros D.Va biplane during the period when Dr.1s were grounded). In March 1918 he brought down eight aircraft in five days, and on 20 April he downed two Camels from 3 Squadron Royal Air Force. Next day Richthofen led 15 Triplanes along the valley of the Somme, where they attacked a pair of R.E.8s before eight Camels from

209 Squadron intervened. Richthofen, patrolling high above as was his custom, saw one Camel break away from the mêlée and nosed over to attack, diving towards the British lines. He poured round after round into the fleeing Camel as they twisted and turned barely 200 feet above the river, and was so distracted with the prospect of his 81st kill that he failed to notice another Camel on his own tail. Captain Roy Brown, a Canadian, opened fire and the red triplane nosed down and hit the ground heavily. Von Richthofen had a single bullet wound through his chest. That night Lieutenant Rhys Davids proposed a toast in the 56 Squadron Mess: 'To our most worthy enemy.'

This Fokker Dr.1 Triplane is a full-size replica built by an American enthusiast and powered by an effectively disguised modern four-cylinder horizontally-opposed aero engine instead of the rotary of the original aircraft.

SPAD Scouts

The great achievements of aviation history have frequently been the progeny of perfect marriages, fortuitous unions of like minds, of men and machines, or of airframes and engines. The French SPAD scouts bear out this notion, for they successfully embodied the talents of two engineers in an airframe/engine combination widely held as the most formidable of the Great War.

SPAD is short for Société Pour L'Aviation et ses Dérivés, a company formed by Louis Blériot in 1914 when he took over his rival Armand Deperdussin's Société Pour les Appareils Deperdussin, contriving a new title to capitalize on a reputation gained by the success of Deperdussin's innovative monoplanes in the 1912 Gordon Bennett Cup and 1913 Coupe Jacques Schneider air races. Perhaps the most valuable asset which Blériot acquired from the near-bankrupt Deperdussin concern, aside from a conveniently-abbreviated name, was the company's technical director Louis Béchéreau, who had been responsible for the midwing monocoque Deperdussin racers which had given France the 200 kilometers per hour speed record and her only ever win in the Schneider event.

Late in 1915, after producing a pair of rotary-engined two-seaters which were less than ecstatically received by France's Aviation Militaire, Béchéreau began

This view of the SPAD XIII shows the midwing wooden braces supporting its landing and flying wires, giving it the appearance of a two-bay biplane.

work on a new single-seat fighter, one eye cast enviously on the efficient watercooled engines which German manufacturers were using. The trouble with aircooled rotaries was that as you drew more power from them the strong gyroscopic forces created by the spinning motor created enormous handling problems for the aeroplane's pilot. At the same time a talented young Swiss named Marc Birkigt, innovative co-founder and chief designer of the Hispano-Suiza motor car company, was developing a watercooled V-8 engine of impressive power/weight ratio. It had an aluminium block, and was lighter and had 500 fewer parts than the German Mercedes engine. A marriage

was arranged between this fine power-plant and a dreadnought of an airframe designed by Béchéreau which offered tremendous structural integrity without the complication, expense and labour-intensity of the tulip-wood monocoque which he had employed in his racers.

With one of Birkigt's 140 hp Hispano-Suizas the first SPAD S.VII flew from the French military airfield at Villacoublay south of Paris in April 1916. It was a compact biplane with unstaggered, di-hedral-less wings of 25-foot span. Its thin section wingribs were set close together for strength, with doubled-up piano-wire bracing and brass-bound interplane struts. The intersections of the flying and

Original, but restored SPAD XIII in the colours of the Lafayette Escadrille (see Indian Head symbol on fuselage side). This version, with a 220hp Hispano-Suiza engine and twin 0.303 Vickers machine guns, first flew in April 1917 and was the favoured mount of French and American aces.

landing wires were supported with wooden braces, giving the S.VII the appearance of a two-bay biplane. It looked and was a tough machine, and despite its greater weight the SPAD performed far better than the Nieuport 17 which was then the mainstay of the Aviation Militaire, having a maximum speed of 122 mph and a climb rate which brought it to 10,000 feet in 15 minutes. The lightly-built Nieuport was prone to structural failure, particularly in high-speed dives. The SPAD would hold together even after combat damage thanks to its structurally dense airframe, and while it lacked the agility of the lighter machines and the twin guns of the German scouts, it provided a steady platform for its single synchronized Vickers 0.303 machine gun.

The first SPAD S.VIIs arrived on the Western Front in September 1916 and were well received by the French *escadrilles de chasse,* whose Nieuport 17s had been outclassed by the German Albatros D.I and D.II scouts. Among the first units to receive the pugnacious new fighter was Groupe de Combat 12, the legendary *Les Cigognes* (storks) whose association with the SPAD led Marc Birkigt to adopt their stylized stork insignia as a radiator mascot on his post-war Hispano-Suiza cars (as a pedestrian-impaler the *cigogne* mascot proved almost as lethal as its namesakes had among the German fliers). Lieutenant Georges Guynemer, lionized young ace of *Les Cigognes* SPA3 squadron, was among the first Aviation Militaire pilots to receive the SPAD following an initial order for 268 machines. By 1917 no fewer than eight French factories were building SPADs faster than any other aeroplane in the world. The air arms of Belgium, Britain, Italy, Russia and the United States wanted them. Five thousand six

hundred S.VIIs were built in France alone, with others manufactured under licence abroad.

But as 1917 came, some of the combat superiority of the SPAD S.VII slipped away to the new Albatros D.R and the Fokker Dr.1 triplane. Marc Birkigt had by this time extracted 150 hp, 180 hp and finally 200 hp from his splendid engine, and Louis Béchéreau capitalized on the increased power availability to further improve his design in the SPAD XII. At Georges Guynemer's suggestion a special S.XII was built with a 37mm Hotchkiss cannon mounted between the cylinder banks of the Hispano-Suiza. They called it *moteur-canon*. The gun fired through a hollow crankshaft and propeller hub which were raised in line with the cannon by way of a geared drive. Guynemer actually managed to down four enemy aircraft with his cannon-firing SPAD, while his *Les Cigognes* colleague

Capitaine René Fonck, the highest scoring Allied ace of the war, scored 11 of his 75 confirmed kills with a *moteur-canon*, but the idea was not a success. There was no positive means of aiming the Hotchkiss except by first firing a trial burst from the Vickers and thus attracting your target's attention. The Hotchkiss was a single-shot weapon which had to be breech-loaded by hand in the cockpit, and its recoil was such that the SPAD would almost be stopped short in the air, delaying pursuit if the first shot had not proved lethal. Cordite fumes from the cannon were another hazard.

While the S.XII was a good idea which faltered in practice, Béchéreau's SPAD XIII was pure genius, combining a 220 hp (later 235 hp) Hispano-Suiza with two 0.303 Vickers guns to give the new SPAD a 30 mph speed advantage over German contemporaries of equivalent firepower. The first S.XIII flew on 4 April 1917 and

Immaculate full-size replica of a SPAD S.VII pictured at an antique aeroplane gathering in the United States. The thin airfoil section and dihedral-less wings are evident in this view.

was immediately rushed into production to replace earlier SPADs and Nieuport 28s. Béchéreau also developed a 300 hp S.XVIII, but it never saw active service, arriving on squadrons just before the Armistice. How well this SPAD might have performed we shall never know, but on hearing that Germany had surrendered, one pilot who had flown the S.XVIII remarked: 'Let the Boche be truly thankful.'

SPADs commanded much respect from those who flew in and against them. Experienced pilots from both sides rate them as the best fighters of World War I. They were also the most numerous. Some 14,400 SPADs were built — more than any other fighter aircraft prior to 1939. Had orders from the United States not been cancelled in peacetime the total would have risen to more than 25,000.

SPADs were, to use the old flier's phrase, 'pilot's aeroplanes'. Here was no forgiving, easy-to-handle machine. They were demanding of their pilots, but like all such aeroplanes, ultimately rewarding and responsive to the skilled touch. An excess of power and the thin airfoil section chosen by Béchéreau for its wings gave the SPAD superior climbing characteristics, but the heavy airframe and that same airfoil accounted for a high sink rate with power off. Glide landings were not recommended: a SPAD needed to be motored in under power. Lack of dihedral on the wings made SPADs especially sensitive to roll control, but the light control forces of the pushrod-operated ailerons took care of that. A SPAD simply had to be flown all the time. It was no machine for 'hands off' flying, but exactly the kind of aeroplane which a talented pilot might exploit to advantage. And they did. René Fonck, of *Les Cigognes* Escadrille SPA103, four times brought down two aircraft in a single day, and once, on 9 May 1918, shot down six German aircraft in two dogfights, three of them in such quick order that their wreckage was all contained in a quarter-mile area. Georges Guynemer, an intense 21-year-old who fought for two years without leave periods, driving himself to the ragged edge of physical and mental fatigue, destroyed 54 German aircraft before disappearing in his SPAD S.XIII on a dawn patrol over Belgium, his loss considered such a blow to the morale of the French populace that the news was witheld from them for a week. In their first six months of flying SPADs, *Les Cigognes* accounted for 200 enemy aircraft destroyed. Béchéreau's beauties were instrumental in restoring mastery of the

air over the Western Front to the Allies and in making the reputations of some of World War I's finest aces. Men like the Italian Maggiore Francesco Barraca, commander of 91a Squadriglia, whose 34 confirmed victories were mostly made in his *Spadas* (the Italian word for Sword which became a popular colloquialism for the SPAD name among Italy's eleven *squadriglie di caccia* equipped with the aircraft). Barraca was a fearsome opponent even against daunting odds. On two occasions he made single-handed attacks on formations of six Austrian fighters, shooting down one each time, and once despatched two Aviatiks within 30 minutes.

America's leading World War I ace Eddie Rickenbacker, who flew with the 94th Aero ('Uncle Sam's Hat-in-Ring') Squadron, declared the SPAD 'the best

ship' he ever flew. 'It was more impressive than any other airplane, any other automobile, any other piece of equipment I had ever seen; the ultimate aircraft in the war . . .' he recalled. Rickenbacker scored 26 victories in eight months.

The SPAD, particularly the S.XIII, was a superb fighting machine. It had speed, manoeuvrability, firepower, and great strength, so that its pilots had no fear of structural failure if they heeled over in a steep dive to pursue or escape a pursuer. The earlier Nieuports had unpleasant habits of losing wing fabric or even entire wings in high speed dives, but Béchéreau's stalwart airframe would hold together under the greatest stress. Its stability made the SPAD a fine gun platform, but it was not entirely without fault. One unendearing little trait was attributable indirectly to Birkigt's powerplant. The header tank for the Hispano-Suiza's cooling system was mounted in the centre section of the upper wing, directly forward of the cockpit and in a perfect position to spray the pilot with scalding water if (as they sometimes did) it sprang a leak or (as happened more often) the tank was punctured in combat. And the SPAD was the very devil to land. Apart from that high sink rate the pilot's position — sitting low down with legs straight out under the engine mount — afforded a poor view ahead, and the aeroplane was fond of ground-looping given half a chance.

Those who mastered the SPAD forgave it all that and more, for here was a marksman's machine, one to stir the blood of a young hunter.

Long fishtail exhausts would have graced one of Marc Birkigt's Hispano-Suiza cars. Close proximity of the centre-section radiator to the pilot's face was the SPAD's least popular feature. Note typical scalloped trailing edge on this S.VII replica.

Sopwith Pup and Camel

'The perfect flying machine,' wrote one Royal Flying Corps pilot of Tommy Sopwith's little Pup. Officially it was known as the Sopwith Scout, but Herbert Smith's compact design bore such a resemblance to his larger 1½ Strutter that the 'Pup' appellation stayed with the aircraft throughout its service. The Pup was trim and remarkably light, weighing in at just 790 lbs empty, so that despite the modest power of its 80 hp Le Rhône rotary engine it could manage a maximum speed of 111 mph — faster than any other aeroplane with that powerplant. Generous wing area and a good power/weight ratio combined to provide fine high-altitude manoeuvrability even after the hour-long climb to the Pup's maximum service ceiling of 17,500 feet. At this heady altitude many scouts became sluggish, mushy and unresponsive, just when their frozen, oxygen-starved pilots least needed recalcitrant aeroplanes. The Pup's nimble, heel-snapping performance soon won it great affection. One RFC test pilot described it as 'the prettiest to look at and the sweetest on the controls of any aeroplane of World War I' — an unequivocal tribute in the face of substantial competition, for he had flown most contemporary British and German aircraft.

The Pup first flew in February 1916. It had a conventional strut-and-wire-braced wooden airframe with fabric covering, ailerons on both upper and lower wings to improve roll rate, and a roomy cockpit whose basketwork seat was uncomfortably hard and left rather too much of a tall pilot's body jutting out into the slipstream, where he was ill protected by a tiny padded windscreen set into the butt of the aeroplane's synchronized Vickers 0.303 machine gun. The single gun was the Pup's major shortcoming. It lacked firepower and the Vickers was uncommonly prone to jamming. That was when the Sopwith's

left
This Sopwith Pup is still flying in England as part of a private collection.

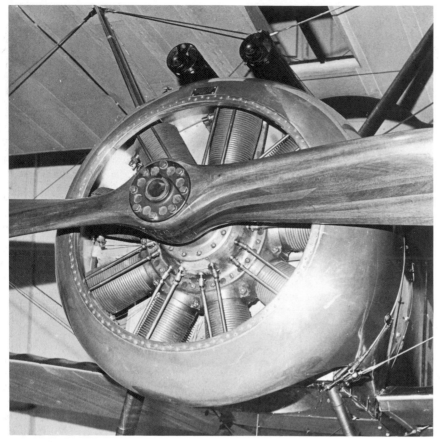

Camels were powered by Gnôme, Le Rhône, Clerget and Bentley rotary engines. This one is the 130hp Clerget, with synchronized twin 0.303 Vickers machine gun installation on a Camel F.1 preserved at the Royal Air Force Museum, Hendon.

The lightly loaded Sopwith Pup would be off the ground in a trice, though forward visibility was poor during take-off.

superior manoeuvrability paid off handsomely by out-turning the enemy and making a swift 'power-dive' for friendly lines. Pilots of 54 Squadron Royal Flying Corps on the Western Front, who seem to have been a particularly musical bunch, composed this little ditty on the subject:

When you soar in the air in your Sopwith Scout,
And you're scrapping with a Hun and your gun cuts out,
Well, you stuff down the nose till your plugs fall out,
'Cos you haven't got a hope in the morning!

The key to painless Pup flying lay in good management of its rotary engine. The engine controls consisted of a hand pump for raising fuel pressure, petrol and air adjustment levers, magneto switch, and an ignition cut-out button, popularly known as the blip switch, on the control column's spade-handle grip. To start the Le Rhône you pumped up fuel pressure until the blow-off valve began to hiss, while the groundcrewman primed each of the nine cylinders with neat petrol from a syringe and hand-turned the engine to suck in the mixture before swinging the propeller as you threw the magneto switch. Provided the priming ritual had been properly performed and you had set the air and fuel settings correctly, the Le Rhône would spin up in a cloud of blue smoke and a waft of the tangy castor oil which fed the engine's total loss lubrication system. Total loss was not exactly right, because much of the castor oil eventually found its way onto the unfortunate pilot in a wind-blown aerosol-like spray. Experienced RFC pilots allegedly counteracted the effects of this unwelcome bath with liberal doses of whisky, though whether the scotch had any therapeutic value is open to doubt. With his engine running smoothly there was little more for a Pup pilot to check before take-off, for his only instruments were an oil pulsometer, air-speed indicator, altimeter, tachometer, compass and spirit-level slip indicator. Once rolling for take-off, his visibility became severely restricted by the nose, upper wing, and not least by the haze of castor oil, but acceleration was so brisk that the lightly laden Pup would invariably be off the ground before an inexperienced pilot was ready for it, climbing away at 50 mph with the wind around that miserable windshield threatening to whip away a loose-fitting pair of flying goggles. The Pup's climb rate brought it to 10,000 feet in under 20 minutes, but the next five thousand took much longer. During protracted climbs to altitude Pup pilots were at greatest risk of attack, and some squadrons took pains to coax every extra foot-per-minute of climb rate from their aeroplanes by stripping them of all unnecessary weight, such as that inefficient but heavy windscreen.

At altitude the Pup's speed was insufficient to give it a combat advantage, but its ability to continue climbing strongly above 10,000 feet and to maintain height even in a whirling dogfight gave it a distinct edge over contemporary German airplanes. James McCudden, VC, noted that 'the Pup

could outmanoeuvre any Albatros no matter how good the German pilot was, and when it came to manoeuvring, the Sopwith could turn twice to the Albatros's once,' while Baron Manfred von Richtofen allowed that he 'saw at once that the enemy aeroplane was superior,' after his flight of three Albatroses encountered a Pup in January 1917.

The Pup's flying controls were light, responsive and well harmonized by the standards of the day, with powerful and effective roll and pitch control. Although its structure was light, the Pup proved capable of sustaining major combat damage and still holding together: one once collided with an Albatros at a closing speed close to 250 mph and returned to base. On another occasion a Pup spun in from 16,000 feet after a machine gun burst blew away an interplane strut and collapsed one lower wing panel. Amazingly its pilot survived, probably because the Pup's light wing loading kept its vertical speed low in the descent.

The first Pups in service arrived at the Western Front late in 1916 in the hands of No. 8 Squadron, Royal Naval Air Service. During their first three months in action the splendid 'Naval Eight' destroyed 14 enemy aircraft and damaged at least another 13. The little Sopwith retained its dominance of the Western Front through much of 1917. In all 1,770 were built, and to the Pup went also the task of making the first ever deck landing, when Squadron Commander E. H. Dunning, Royal

Running up the Le Rhône rotary engine on one of two Sopwith Pups still flying in England. Note the ring sight for the Pup's single 0.303 Vickers machine gun.

Navy, set his Pup down on H.M.S. *Furious* on 2 August 1917. A few days later poor Dunning drowned when a gust blew his Pup overboard before *Furious'* deck crew could catch hold of the aeroplane.

The Sopwith Camel also won affection from its pilots and rivals, but tempered with caution and respect, for it was no docile Pup. So named because of its hump-backed profile, the Camel emerged as the most successful combat aircraft of the Great War, accounting for more than 2,790 enemy aircraft in less than two years' service, a record not nearly matched by any other scout. Nor did any other type terrify or kill so many inexperienced pilots, for the Camel could be as lethal to those who mishandled it as its two 0.303 Vickers machine guns could be to an enemy.

The Camel's combat performance and its reputation as a pilot-biter stemmed from the extraordinary manoeuvrability afforded by the concentration of its main masses (engine, guns and ammunition, fuel tank and pilot) in the forward seven feet of the fuselage, creating, in the words of one Camel pilot, 'a gyroscope with wings'. The strong gyroscopic forces of the Camel's powerful rotary engine (they were powered variously by 110 hp Le Rhône, 150 hp Bentley, or most common-ly 130 hp Clerget engines), combined with the mass concentration, made the aeroplane uniquely responsive in turns, but such were the forces created by the spinning engine and propeller that the Camel's control surfaces were sometimes unable to compensate, particularly if mishandled. The Camel was unstable in all axes, and especially sensitive in pitch. Thus the aeroplane had the makings of a superlative dogfighter which could turn almost in its own length and make the speediest changes in direction of any contemporary aircraft. Yet in unwary hands those same qualities could turn the Camel into a death-trap. The gyrosopic forces were such that turns to left or right both required *left* rudder. A left turn against the gyro action of the engine was ponderously slow. A right turn going with the action was instant and snappy, so that many pilots preferred to turn right through 270 degrees if they wanted to go left! Firm rudder control was a must in the Camel, but since the direction of rudder deflection was often the opposite to that expected many inexperienced Camel pilots ended up in spins, especially if they suddenly applied power to the rotating engine at low airspeed close to a stall. The gyroscopic force would simply snap the aeroplane over into a spin, and at that time little was known about spinning or recovery.

Equally fearsome was the Camel's apparent inability to be recovered from

This Pup is one of a number fitted with a variety of skid undercarriages for deck take-off and landing trials aboard Royal Navy ships late in 1917.

'The prettiest to look at and the sweetest on the controls of any aeroplane of World War I'. Note that ineffective padded windscreen behind the Vickers gun installation.

inverted flight. After a succession of fatalities in which Camels dived inverted into the ground, rumours grew that once upside-down the aircraft became stabilized. So strongly did these rumours blossom that the Camel's safety was questioned in Parliament, and all stunting on the aeroplane was banned by the Royal Flying Corps and Royal Naval Air Service. The truth, as ever, was less dramatic. Many of the upside-down crashes had been caused by the pilots suddenly applying forward (nose-down) stick. The Camel's pitch sensitivity brought an instant response, and the brief moment of negative g was sufficient to catapult the occupant clean out of the cockpit. Although, as Captain Roy Brown noted, 'the spade-handled stick is strong enough to hang on to if the aeroplane gets inverted', few such luckless fliers were able to scramble back in time, and soon the RFC Flying Notes for Camel tyros carried a stern warning to 'always wear a belt or harness as there is a tendency to leave the seat when diving vertically.'

Mastery of the Camel rewarded the skilled flier with an aircraft which came as close as possible to being an extension of his own body. The peculiarities which were the bane of the unwary could be turned to advantage in a dogfight, and unlike its predecessor the Camel was not lacking in firepower. Two 0.303 Vickers with Constantinesco hydraulic interrupter gear gave a rapid rate of fire from two 500-round belts of ammunition, and a double gun jam was rare, so there was rarely a need to turn and run, provided ammunition lasted. Captain Henry Woollett, seventh highest-scoring Camel ace with 30 victories in the aircraft while serving with 43 Squadron RFC in France, declared that his Camel could 'dictate any fight and turn inside any scout the enemy

used'. His technique was to patrol at an altitude around 12,000 feet, where the Camel performed best, waiting for enemy aircraft to come to him. Although the Camel could climb on up to its service ceiling of 19,000 feet the heavier machine did not have the Pup's sprightly performance at altitude and lost some of its superior manoeuvrability up high.

Not only was the Camel the King of Combat in World War I, but one particular aircraft set a personal record as a Hun Killer. Major William George Barker, VC, DSO, MC, a Canadian officer, destroyed 33 enemy aircraft, nine kite balloons and sent a further six aircraft out of control in his Camel No. B6313 in a year's operational flying. Perhaps significant in Barker's tally was his refusal to use the Vickers guns' standard Aldis sight. Instead he fixed two steel bars across the muzzles and breeches of his guns and cut notches in them for sighting. Evidently it worked well.

Away from the pressure of combat the uncrowned king of the Camel was one Captain D. V. Armstrong, who flew with 78 Squadron RFC from Suttons Farm on the outskirts of London. Armstrong perfected the once-outlawed sport of 'Camelbatics', specializing in ultra-low-level aerobatics. He would loop from take-off and use the gyroscopic forces of the engine to flick-roll his Camel at ground level. On at least one occasion he brushed a wingtip in the grass as the Camel gyrated round its horizontal spin. Armstrong finally was killed in a Camel stunting accident just two weeks before the Armistice.

Once a Camel pilot, always a Camel pilot, went the old Royal Flying Corps saying. If you learned to respect its ways and to master its peculiarities the Camel was a most willing and very able weapon.

De Havilland Moth

The Neiman-Marcus store in Dallas, Texas, is the only shop I know where you can find aeroplanes alongside life's less exotic needs. But had you been strolling down London's Oxford Street in the late 1920s you might have been surprised to find a trim little biplane forming the window display of a department store. The biplane was a de Havilland Moth, or *Moff*, in the Cockney twang of the many young boys who pressed their noses against the store windows for a better view. Pronounce it as you will, the name was one which soon fell easily from the lips of people who had never been within thousands of miles of Oxford Street.

'I did not feel it was suitable or good sales policy to give it only a numeral,' explained the biplane's creator Captain (later Sir) Geoffrey de Havilland, 'and my enthusiasm for natural history led me to seek the solution in entomology. It suddenly struck me that the name Moth was just right.'

Just how right quickly became apparent after Captain de Havilland first flew his D.H. 60 Moth from Stag Lane Aerodrome on the northern fringe of London on 22 February 1925. Here was a cheap, easy to fly, simple to operate aeroplane which personified de Havilland's dream of an 'aeroplane for all', a runabout which ordinary folk might fly as nonchalantly as they drove motor cars. Encouraged by a vigorous publicity campaign Moth fever took hold of a population ill-able to afford motor cars, let alone aeroplanes. Within three months of its first flight, Alan Cobham had taken the Moth on a round trip to Switzerland in a day, flying from Croydon to Zurich and back, 1,000 miles, in under 14 hours — an impressive demonstration of the aeroplane's practicality.

The Moth design was of the utmost simplicity: plywood-skinned, box-section fuselage, fabric-covered, wooden flying surfaces with wings which could be folded alongside for storage or road-towing, and a 60 hp ADC Cirrus four-cylinder in-line engine which de Havilland's chief engineer, Major Frank Halford, had created from one half of a

Perhaps best-known of all Moths was the D.H.82A Tiger Moth which was the Royal Air Force's basic trainer during World War II and is still flying in some numbers. This one is part of a flying club fleet in southern England.

top
The classic D.H.60G Gipsy Moth, this example restored in the colours of Amy Johnson's famous *Jason*, though bearing the name of owner Ron Souch's wife *Joan*. Interwoven 'DH' symbol on the wheel hub covers was another de Havilland trade mark.

above
Sir Geoffrey de Havilland.

war-surplus 120 hp Airdisco-Renault V-8. The Moth was, as one newspaper put it, 'an aeroplane for youth', and to inspire Britain's youth to air-mindedness, the visionary Director of Civil Aviation, Sir Sefton Brancker — later to die tragically in the crash of the airship R-101 — ordered 90 Moths for the new government-sponsored flying clubs. It was 'Branks' too who encouraged a young Yorkshire typist when she wrote to him in 1930 begging support for a madcap scheme — a solo flight from England to Australia. Ten weeks later Amy Johnson's Moth *Jason* landed at Darwin after her 10,000 mile journey. It hangs today in the Science Museum in London.

The original 60 hp Moth was developed through successive power-plant changes, the most popular engines being the 85 hp and 90 hp Cirrus II and III and the Gipsy series, developed by Frank Halford when supplies of surplus Airdiscos dwindled. Gipsy engines, ranging from 100 hp to 145 hp, powered every Moth from the D.H. 60G Gipsy Moth to the best-known of all, the D.H. 82 Tiger Moth, beloved and accursed mentor of hundred of thousands of student pilots over five decades from its first appearance in 1931.

De Havilland set up a worldwide network of sales and service stations for Moths, where you could buy your machine, be taught to fly it (one enterprising dealer promised to teach you in a single day) and have it maintained. At the company's Stag Lane headquarters you could even rent a 'Moth Garage' for one pound per week, and have DH ground staff prepare your aeroplane for flight on the strength of a telephone call before you motored out to the airfield.

In 1925 a basic Moth cost £885, but the economies of large-scale production (16 per week by 1929) soon brought the price down to £730 for an 85 hp Cirrus II-engined Moth, including a tool kit, engine, cockpit and propeller covers, and a choice of colour scheme: red or blue-doped fuselage with silver wings and tail surfaces. A de luxe model came complete with sets of wheel chocks, a tailskid trolley and even a shooting stick in its baggage compartment. Maintenance, promised the de Havilland literature, was so simple that your Moth could 'be kept in perfect order by anybody with only ordinary knowledge of motor cars', and was in any case available at the factory for modest fixed rates. The engine was 'as straightforward as a motorcycle engine, robust and reliable, and does not require skilled attention. It runs on commercial brands of petrol and oil which can be obtained from any wayside garage'. The sight of a Moth filling up at a roadside petrol station was not uncommon. To prove the reliability of the Gipsy engine de Havilland sealed an engine and flew it for 600 hours without maintenance save for routine tappet-greasing and oil replenishment. The Gypsy covered 50,000 miles in nine months. Replacement parts at overhaul time cost £7 2s 11d.

'Anyone can learn to fly a Moth in a few hours, its controls are easy to master and simple to operate,' the Moth brochure boasted. 'Any open field is a potential aerodrome. The Moth leaves the ground with pilot, passenger and luggage after a run of only a hundred yards.' Left to its own devices a Moth would take-off on its own, as the pioneer pilot and round-the-world yachtsman Sir Francis Chichester discovered in 1929. Thinking that the professional pilot accompanying him was handling the take-off, Chichester folded his arms and waited. So did his companion. The Gipsy Moth climbed away unperturbed, and later went on to carry Chichester solo to Australia, New Zealand and across the Pacific to Japan.

The Gipsy was certainly a less demanding machine than the Tiger Moth, which was developed from the steel-tube fuselaged D.H. 60T to meet an Air Ministry requirement for a Royal Air Force trainer. Although the D.H. 60 series were popular with civilian operators, the Ministry was unhappy with the front cockpit location directly beneath the centre-section fuel tank and between the cabane struts, making entry and exit

trim lawns set for afternoon teas. But Geoffrey de Havilland's aspirations for the people's aeroplane, which would get the man in the street off the street and into the sky, never really came to fruition. Flying in the 1930s was as much an élitist pastime as it is today, restricted by high cost to those who could afford it or those (like Amy Johnson) prepared to sacrifice other pursuits in order to finance a grand obsession. Even the cheapest new Moth cost four or five times the price of a small family car; the ratio holds good for modern light aeroplanes.

Before flying, the Moth's wings must first be unfurled by disengaging their catches, swinging them out to the spread position and engaging the locking bolts, leather retaining straps and jury struts, so the Moth emerges from its slumber as its namesake from a chrysalis. Boarding from the Gipsy Moth's starboard side the

(particularly a hurried exit when necessary) difficult for a pilot in full service flying clothing and parachute. De Havilland's chief designer Arthur Hagg re-engineered the airframe with a new 120 hp Gipsy III inverted in-line engine, moved the centre-section forwards, swept the wings back and thus serendipitously created a legendary aeroplane. When Tiger Moth production finally ceased in August 1945, 9,231 had been built in Britain, Australia, Canada, New Zealand, Norway, Portugal and Sweden.

A ride in a Moth is a time-warp journey back to the genteel days of pre-war aero club flying, to grass airfields whose runways were always into the wind, and white-fenced clubhouses with

reason for the Air Ministry's strictures becomes immediately apparent: to reach the front cockpit you must clamber through a cat's cradle of struts and wires. It cannot be rushed. The Moth must be soloed from the rear cockpit, but in either position you must remember not to let your left hand trawl lazily over the port side of the cockpit, or the long exhaust pipe which carries the Gipsy engine's note off towards the tail will issue a blistering reminder. That pipe serves as an efficient cockpit heater, and the upright, partially-exposed engine also wafts warm air back, making the Gipsy Moth's accommodation more comfortable than the chill pits of a Tiger Moth, where your body is assailed by vicious darts of

Moths were sold in every part of the globe. This is the Canadian Moth headquarters in the late 1920s.

A rare bird indeed is this American-built de Havilland D.H.60M Moth, manufactured in 1929. It differs from contemporary British-built Moths in having a welded steel tube fuselage frame instead of a wooden structure. The star emblem was a Moth trade mark.

icy air from all quarters even on balmy days.

The reliable, low-compression Gipsy engine can usually be depended upon to start first swing. No brakes, just a fixed tailskid to slow the Moth by tearing out great chunks of grass, so the prudent pilot has someone at each wingtip to help swing her into the wind. The Gipsy's tail comes up very quickly under take-off power, and there is little swing to counteract before she's off at 45 mph and settling into an unhurried 80 mph cruise. Trimming the Gipsy (or Tiger) Moth is accomplished with a 'cheese-cutter' lever on the port side of the cockpit, which alters the tension of springs attached to the control column, adjusting longitudinal trim without recourse to tabs or variable-incidence tailplanes, though some pilots claim that the DH system mars the feel of the Moths because one is always pulling or pushing against spring tension.

Inter-cockpit communication, unless the Moth has been kitted out with a modern electric intercom system which horrifies purists, is by the time-honoured Gosport tube, developed from its Avro 504 days to a peak of efficiency, if that is the right word for a device resembling a doctor's stethoscope through which your

instructor somehow managed to hammer home the rudiments of airmanship as you strained your ears to catch the bathwater gurglings of the instrument. It was said that you could always identify an experienced Moth instructor by the black ring left on his face by the Gosport's rubber mouthpiece.

In calm air the Moth is a delight, inherently stable, perhaps even a little too stable laterally, for the ailerons are heavy and none too effective thanks to differential gearing which slows the movement of the down-going aileron to prevent adverse yaw. The differential ailerons were also adopted as a safety measure, to roll the Moth level if it was stalled in a turn. Handley-Page automatic slots on the top wing also dampen the effects of a stall, creeping out at about 60 mph as the wings' angle of attack increases, until the Moth stalls at around 40 mph. The Gipsy Moth's slots are fully automatic with no pilot control: on the Tiger Moth they could be locked in the closed position for aerobatics.

When approaching to land, or manoeuvring close to the ground, a Moth pilot could monitor his airspeed without looking into the cockpit, because Moths had two airspeed indicators — a conventional instrument on the panel, and

The Gipsy Moth's long exhaust pipe keeps the open cockpits heated nicely, but beware of trailing a hand over the cockpit side!

out on the port interplane strut a calibrated metal plate across which a spring-loaded pointer was moved by air pressure.

To prove his company's claim that 'landing a Moth could not be easier', Geoffrey de Havilland used to demonstrate approaches with the throttle fully closed and the stick held right back as the Moth floated down safely at 40 mph to a perfect three-pointer. Until one day his Moth's long-suffering undercarriage gave way with a great c r u-u-u-n-c-h, unfortunately when a photographer happened to be present to capture the moment. Amy Johnson was noted for hard 'arrivals' in her Moth, and Sefton Brancker, who learned to fly and had his personal Moth as Director of Civil Aviation, was the butt of many jokes for his poor landings. Once, when he was arriving as a passenger with another pilot, the Moth bounced hard, and as it taxied up to the waiting reception committee Brancker was heard to remark: 'They'll probably blame me for that!'

Geoffrey de Havilland's 'Moths for every purse and purpose' were the most practical and successful British light aeroplanes ever built. Not Aeroplanes for All, perhaps, but assuredly aeroplanes for all time.

Simplicity was the keynote of the Gipsy Moth's cockpit. The funnel-shaped device is the speaking tube for the Gosport 'inter-cockpit communication system'.

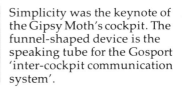

Ford Tri Motor

The cheek of it! Imagine! Here's this former journalist now aircraft engineer William Bushnell Stout bouncing back after the rejection of his torpedo-bomber design by the US Navy with a circular letter to the captains of American industry asking for one thousand dollars apiece to fund another project. 'And I can only promise you one thing,' he wrote. 'You will probably never see the money again!'

Who could have blamed Edsel Ford if he had screwed up that letter when it arrived on his desk back in 1923? But he didn't. Instead he wrote out a cheque for $1,000 and persuaded his father Henry to do the same. Thus was formed a partnership which was to link the Ford name with the development of air transport in the United States in the 1930s and led to the creation of a legendary airliner — the Ford Tri Motor.

Bill Stout (friends called him 'Jacknife') was not a total unknown when he mailed out his fund-raising flier, indeed he had pioneered all-metal aircraft construction in the United States, but the tri-motor 3-AT Air Pullman which the Stout Metal Airplane Company built in a factory provided by Ford can scarcely have convinced father and son that they had invested wisely. It was little short of a disaster: ugly, impractical, short on any saving grace. When Ford's test pilot 'Shorty' Shroeder flew it in November 1925 he walked away from the 3-AT without a backward glance. Ford called it a monstrosity and sent Stout off into that limbo of those fallen from grace — a nationwide lecture tour. A factory fire obligingly destroyed the aeroplane and every piece of paperwork relating to it, and Henry Ford appointed a new design committee headed by speedboat designer Harold Hicks to try to salvage something from the ruins. Ford did not like flying, but he recognized the role which air transport was to play. 'The airplane is going to enlarge the work of the automobile,' he declared. 'The motor car has mixed people up so thoroughly that one can hardly fool any American anymore about any part of his own country. But they can be fooled about other parts of the world. The airplane will stop all that.'

The vehicle of this transportation revolution first flew on 11 June 1926. Though it had three engines the Model 4-AT (for Air Transport) bore scant resemblance to Stout's original design save for its corrugated Alclad skinning, which was to earn Fords the nickname Flying Washboard. Ford was still sceptical about the project, to the extent that he would not allow his name or the company logo to appear on the prototype until it was proven successful.

He did not have long to wait. The all-metal 4-AT soon entered production and was readily accepted by an eager public. Legend has it that the design — certainly its wing section — was inspired by the Fokker F.VII tri-motor which Commander Richard Byrd used for his Ford-sponsored North Pole Expedition in 1925-26. When Byrd flew the Fokker to Dearborn to visit the Fords, Henry is supposed to have instructed his men to go over every inch of it with tape measures, then told them: *build me one like that, only make it in metal.*

Ironically, Ford-fever caught on strongest with American air travellers at a time when public confidence in wooden aeroplanes had plunged along with the wreckage of a tri-motor Fokker which disintegrated in a storm, killing Notre Dame University's idolised football coach Knute Rockne. Thereafter the promise of a metal aeroplane which would not break was a major selling point, and it was a promise that the Ford Tri Motor made and kept: no Ford ever suffered an inflight structural failure, or has to this day.

The 4-At was powered by a trio of 224 hp Wright Whirlwind engines, giving a maximum speed of 130 mph and a cruise of nearly 100 mph, which was faster than any contemporary airliner. The six-foot-high passenger cabin, tastefully decorated in colour-toned Ford Aero Board, had cane-backed seats for 11/12 passengers, reading lights, big panoramic windows of non-shattering glass, even curtains. Passengers loved it. Early customers included National Air Transport (later to become United Airlines), which introduced the Ford on its New York-Chicago route, Bill Stout (!), who formed his own airline in Michigan, a Los Angeles auto dealer named Jack Maddux who started an air route between Los Angeles and San Francisco, and the Royal Typewriter company, which used a specially adapted 4-AT as a flying showroom. It could carry 210 Royal typewriters, and used to drop 62 of them by parachute through a special chute. What it did for the typewriters I cannot imagine, but a Ford could stand up to anything you threw at it or out of it. A stout aeroplane, if not a Stout one, as witness the fate of a Ford 4-AT flown by

Ford's old friend Richard Byrd, who took the aeroplane over the South Pole in 1929 and abandoned it buried in snow at his Little America base in Antartica. Years later he returned, dug the Ford out, ran its engines and flew it away. You can see it today in the Ford Museum in Dearborn, Michigan.

From the 4-AT was developed the 5-AT, slightly larger all round, with a 15-seat passenger cabin and three 420 hp Pratt & Whitney Wasp engines which offered modest performance improvements but nearly doubled the Ford's payload for much the same operating costs. The $55,000 5-AT inaugurated Transcontinental Air Transport's (now TWA) coast-to-coast service. It was strictly a trip for masochists. Westbound journeys took 28 hours. Return flights, against the prevailing winds, 31 hours. But going by Ford was still the fastest way to cross America.

The Ford, or Tin Goose if you prefer its most poular of many nicknames, was an extraordinary success. Though out of production (198 were built) before the 'modern' airliners such as Boeing's 257 or the Douglas DC-2 entered service,

Few Tin Geese remained as immaculate as this factory-bright Ford 5-AT, built in March 1932 for a customer in Colombia. The beautiful engine-turned 'birds-eye' finish on the propeller blades was an optional extra, as were the sculptured wheelpants. Note the external control fulcrums and wires leading from the outside cockpit wall through the wing root.

'One More Tri' is not an original Ford aircraft but a modern version of the Tri Motor built by Charles LeMaster in the United States, still retaining the distinctive corrugated skin of the Tin Goose.

Tri Motors continued to haul loads throughout the world into the 1970s. Indeed they still do: Island Airways operating out of Port Clinton, Ohio, still uses one for inter-island services, and Scenic Airways of Las Vegas, Nevada, will show you the beckoning neon of the high-rollers' mecca from the cabin of a Ford, just for nostalgia's sake.

How did Ford passengers travel? Noisily and none too comfortably, I'm afraid. Three uncowled, radial engines blattering away, exposed elevator and rudder control cables which slapped against its corrugated flanks, wrinkled skin which rattled and 'oil-canned', and the lack of soundproofing made a Tin Goose a noisy bird indeed. Sitting in the winged washboard's cabin could offer all the comfort of a tin hut in a storm. A trip through heavy rain or hail afforded passengers all the acoustic bliss of a Spike Jones album in quadraphonic sound. Cabin attendants gave you a wad of cotton wool when you boarded to ward off the Goose's worst excesses, but you had to bring you own coats or blankets to cope with the biting cold of the early unheated models. Even the heated cabins were only moderately better. A Ford was always either too cold or uncomfortably hot, and the absence of seatbelts in some aircraft, combined with summertime turbulence at the low altitudes at which Fords flew,

made air-sickness a way of life. 'There was much more air-sickness then than there is now,' a former Ford hostess recalled, 'and ventilation was pretty crude. There were heated planes, but in order to rid the cabin of exhaust fumes we turned the heat off and then wrapped in blankets. In looking back I wonder why anybody rode at all.'

One reason was the Tri Motor's sturdy, reassuring appearance. That great thick wing, devoid of fussy struts and bracing, looked so strong. It *was* strong. Ford engineers allegedly drove a truck over it to test its strength. Three engines promised security. The Ford could fly comfortably on two: some pilots used to shut down the centre engine for economy on long trips to avoid a fuel stop. It would stay aloft on just one. Here was an aeroplane built like a boxcar, clad in a rust-resistant sandwich of duralumin and aluminium, designed to the same low-maintenance philosophy of that other popular Ford product, the Model T. A standard Ford service depot kit for the Tri Motor reflects the undemanding nature of its maintenance requirements: screwdriver, pliers, tinsnips, chisel, rawhide mallet, files, wrenches, rivet gun, ball-pein hammer, plumb bob, drills, paintbrushes. One South American pilot hauling oil drilling equipment in his Ford broke its back in a rough landing with an

Wicker-seats, overhead coat racks, curtains and individual reading lights were standard features on early Ford 4-ATs. This one was operated by Transcontinental Air Transport, now Trans World Airlines.

overload (overloading a Ford was standard operating procedure among the cargo-carriers who flew them when the airlines gave way to passengers' demands for more speed). His ground crew repaired it on site with hand tools and they flew it away.

There was more than just Model T philosophy in the Tri Motor. Those big round wooden control wheels? That's right. Straight from the de luxe Model T production line, where they were called steering wheels. And you needed a big wheel to saw away at at times, because the Ford's controls were heavy muscle-builders, especially in turbulence. All the more remarkable that a barnstormer named Harold S. Johnson used one of these six-ton aluminium elephants for an aerobatic routine, performing a six-turn spin, snap and slow rolls and hammer-head stalls, finishing up with three consecutive loops from ground level with the centre engine shut down, and a 'Tennes-see Waltz' landing the rocking Ford from one mainwheel to the other. The elevator trim wheel in a Ford took 62 turns from one extreme to the other, there were three throttles to juggle (perhaps that is why Johnson shut down one motor) and aero-batics were far from the minds of the Tri Motor's designers. Johnson must have been a remarkable man. Another barn-stormer, one Ben F. Gregory, had a 4-AT decked out with a battery of 12 floodlights shining through its open windows. He would perform a spectacular night aerobatic routine with his 'Ship From Mars' to the accompaniment of a firework display.

Pilots from rival companies used to say that airlines using Fords hired all their crews from freak shows at circuses, this slight arising from the old saw that

you needed three hands to fly a Tri Motor. There was some truth in it, not just because you had three throttles and mixture controls to contend with. During landing, for example, a Ford pilot might have to juggle engines, heave the lumbering Tri Motor about with his steering wheel, and then be ready to battle with a device between the seats called a Johnson Bar, which worked the brakes. Aside from its irritating habit of catching on uniform jackets and tearing cuffs, this bar called for some dexterity. Pulling back applied brake to both wheels; movement to either side applied differential brake, though some Fords had a rudder couple whereby pulling back on the Johnson Bar and deflecting the rudder pedals would give braking in the desired direction. A Ford man also needed good eyesight to monitor the health of the wing-mounted engines, whose vital signs were recorded by instruments mounted out on the nacelles, not on the panel, and if he was wise he would also have availed himself of the cotton wool ration. Many Tri Motor pilots suffered poor hearing after years of service in Tin Geese.

Like its crinkly skin when fresh from the factory, the Ford Tri Motor shone brightly in the pioneering era of American air travel and continued to shine long after its polish had dulled carrying formidable loads in the world's inhospit-able regions, its cabin filled with everything from bloody cattle carcasses to freshly-mined coal.

I once overheard a little boy standing behind me in a queue for a joyride in a Ford Tri Motor ask his mother why the aeroplane had all those wrinkles in its grey skin. *Because it's old like me*, mum told him. Nonsense. The Tin Goose is ageless.

A Ford 5-AT restored in the colours of American Airlines, which operated this aircraft on transcontinental services in the 1930s.

Beech
Staggerwing

In 1924 Walter Beech, Clyde Cessna and Lloyd Stearman set themselves up as the Travel Air Company on the windy plains of Kansas. They built sturdy, dependable biplanes and vast single-engined monoplanes which looked like scaled-up imitations of Charles Lindbergh's New York-Paris Ryan. One, named *Woolaroc*, was flown by barnstomer Art Goebel to first place in the disastrous 1927 Dole Derby Race from San Francisco to Honolulu. It was no mean achievement, for all but two of the competitors in that doleful derby crashed.

Travel Air was doing nicely but, like all creative men, the trio grew restless and eager for change. Lloyd Stearman went first. Clyde Cessna followed a year later, convinced that his future lay in monoplanes. He was right. Every one of the 170,000 aeroplanes delivered by the Cessna Aircraft Company has been a monoplane.

Walter Beech sold out to the Curtiss-Wright company, but stayed with Travel Air to supervise development of the Mystery Ship racers which captured hundreds of transcontinental speed records in the 1920s, then he too moved on, setting up shop across town in Wichita as the Beech Aircraft Company, in April 1932.

Beech and his chief designer Ted Wells were diehard biplane men. They knew they had one last two-winger in them, and their plan was nothing if not ambitious. They would build a biplane that would fly at 200 mph, land at a safe 60 mph and go faster, higher and further than the monoplanes their rivals were building. It would be a masterpiece.

And so it was: an exquisite four-place cabin biplane with a tightly-cowled 420 hp Wright Whirlwind radial engine, streamlined wheelpants with semi-retractable wheels and an extraordinary

An early 1934 view of Staggerwing production at the Beech factory in Wichita. The aircraft in the foreground is the monstrous 690hp Wright Cyclone-engined Model A17F once owned by Howard Hughes.

back-staggered wing configuration last seen on the British Airco DH.5 fighter in 1917. This negative stagger wing configuration, with the upper wing set behind the lower in reverse of traditional biplane practice, had a triple advantage: it offered good pilot visibility, since the upper wing did not obstruct upward and forward vision as on conventional biplanes; the forward location of the lower wing enabled it, rather than the fuselage, to be used for mounting the landing gear; and there was the aerodynamic bonus of having the upper wing's centre of lift behind the centre of gravity, while that of the lower wing was ahead of it. When approaching the stall the lower wing gives up flying while the upper is still producing lift. The rearward centre of lift then pitches the aircraft down and it picks up flying speed again. The Staggerwing's stall is docile, particularly for such a high performance airplane.

Beech's new Model 17R was everything he had hoped it would be. Above all else it was fast, almost embarrassingly so, for even the best US Army pursuit ships of the day were hard-pressed to match its top speed of 201 mph. The Beechcraft was the only production lightplane ever to have outperformed its military contemporaries, then or since.

That the year 1932 was one of eeconomic gloom and that buyers were not exactly banging down his door seemed to matter little to Walter Beech. He had working capital from the disposal of Travel Air, and although he had proved conclusively that a properly-designed biplane could outrun a monoplane, he pressed the point by advertising an even more powerful, faster and more expensive aeroplane — the Model A17F, which had a masive Cyclone engine of no less than 690 hp and cruised at 250 mph. It looked like a pugnacious bumble bee,

Typical smoky start-up from the 450hp Pratt & Whitney Wasp radial engine of a D-17S Staggerwing. Coil-spring undercarriage suspension is evident in this picture.

57

but was more like a bear to handle on the ground. The A17F would chase its own tail in a vicious groundloop if you did not handle the throttle and rudder very carfully on take-off. Landings they say, were all but uncontrollable and best accomplished with closed eyes, a firm grip on something and a fervent prayer.

Amazingly an order came in for this $18,000 airplane, and once Beech's engineers had solved the problem of weld-joints breaking under the Cyclone's punishing vibrations the A17F was delivered to Sanford Textiles, makers of the fashionable Palm Beach suits. A second A17FS with a 710 hp Cyclone was bought by Howard Hughes as a trainer for his record-breaking H-1 racer.

His quest for pure speed indulged, Beech began attuning his aeroplane more closely to the market. First came a more economical engine of 225 hp, and to preserve some of that spectacular performance he arranged for the landing gear to retract, a rarity in biplanes. So the new Model B17L took on the unique, classic lines of the Staggerwing, a name coined by a Miami airshow commentator in 1935 but never officially adopted (or used at all by purists: *call it a Model 17 or just a Beechcraft,* they say).

I have coveted Staggerwings ever since I saw a picture of one in my *Boy's Book of Aircraft.* I have read about them, studied photographs, built models, but never so much as caught a glimpse of one

until about six years ago when a friend telephoned to say there was a Beech 17 at a local airfield. This aeroplane was a Model D17S built in 1943 for the United States Army Air Force. The D17S with a 450 hp Pratt & Whitney R-958 Wasp Junior engine was the most numerous of all, used during World War II by the USAAF, US Navy and British Royal Navy as a communications aircraft and VIP transport.

Misguided people may try to tell you that a Staggerwing Beech is ugly. Pay no heed. It is perhaps the most beautiful of all biplanes, along with the Hawker High Speed Fury and Waco SRE, a sculpture of curves and ellipses which has scarcely a straight line, as if rough-hewn from stone and left to the Kansas winds to be smoothed and fashioned to perfection. When you step aboard through the single rear door you are transported back half a century by that heady scent of old aeroplane, subtle blends of worn leather, dope, oil, gasoline and purest nostalgia.

There is so much *room* in a Staggerwing: a wide bench in the rear for three, and individual seats up front of soft, rich brown leather. If your passengers were the nervous sort you could order your aeroplane with individual parachutes fitted into the upholstery. The Staggerwing's sumptuous cabin is enclosed in a solidly-built airframe of welded steel tube and huge steel trusses, with two-spar wooden

Most numerous of Staggerwing models was the 450hp Pratt & Whitney Wasp-engined Model D17S pictured here.

Walter Beech pictured with a 225hp Jacobs-engined B17L in August 1934. The B17L model was the first Staggerwing to have a retractable undercarriage.

wings whose ribs are set just six inches apart. The beauty is more than fabric-deep, indeed it gives the impression of being a machine you might fly into something substantial and expect to walk away from.

The cockpit is pure 1930s, with a haphazard collection of cranks, levers, taps, knobs and warning lights placarded with varying degrees of advice, caution, instruction and consolation, and a massive half-moon control-wheel mounted on Beech's familiar 'throwover' arm so that the aeroplane may be flown from either seat, just like the modern Bonanzas and Barons.

Starting Pratt & Whitney radial engines is much like firing up one of those old steam traction engines — all coaxing, cajoling and cursing. Bring them to the boil at just the right time and they never fail you. But get it wrong and they sulk huffily at your fumblings and wait in dumb silence for you to try again. Ideally the Staggerwing pilot needs three hands for this starting ceremony. One raises fuel pressure with a wobble pump, whilst the others dance about the panel selecting fuel taps, master switch, magnetos, mixture, throttle, keep on with that pumping, give her a few shots of prime, pause, hit the starter and yes, there's a whine, an asthmatic wheeze, and one, two, three spatulate blades of the big Hamilton Standard controllable propeller flick past and an artillery barrage breaks out below. The blades mesh and disappear, and so does the lower wing, in an oily fog of brown-grey smoke. The Pratt & Whitney rumbles away in deep bass as you start out. However delightful in the air, a Staggerwing on the ground is a morose and uncooperative beast,

impatient to get into the air. So it sulks, and won't go where you want it to, and you cannot see clearly where it is going because that big round engine blocks your forward view. You snake along, weaving left and right with your head out of the open window to check that you are headed in the right direction. The ride is nice though, soft and bouncy on the aeroplane's coil-spring landing gear, *boing-boing-boing* across bumps and hillocks like a child on a pogo stick.

There is no sound quite like that of a 450 hp Pratt & Whitney Wasp at take-off power. Conversation is impossible, but the Staggerwing is off the ground in a trice and the noise subsides as the landing gear clunks up beneath the cabin floor. The biplane climbs with little effort at 1,500 feet per minute and will go five miles high if you wish. It will fly at 180 mph and travel nearly 1,000 miles in five hours with five people and their baggage in comfort seldom found, then land at tiny grass fields that modern light-planes with similar load and performance capabilities could never look at. The American writer Tom Mayer claims once to have carried nine people in his Staggerwing, out of a hot and high airstrip in Mexico. Small wonder that the military dubbed their Beech 17s 'Travellers'.

The Staggerwing is much more than just another old-time biplane. Its airframe, though nearly 50 years old, is so cleanly designed that it is reluctant to slow up, and sails down at a 15:1 glide ratio power off, which is better than some gliders. The pilot's manual even recommends a 500-foot *climb* as the first course of action in the event of an engine failure, trading excess airspeed for altitude while

Final production model Staggerwing was the G-17S. This aircraft was the first G-17S to be delivered and was operated by the West Indies Sugar Corporation in the Dominican Republic.

you sort things out. Such techniques are usually the prerogative of the fighter pilot.

But the Staggerwing's handling could fool you into thinking that it was a fighter. The controls are ball-bearing hinged and cable operated. Just hint at what you would like the aeroplane to do and it does it. The ailerons in particular are famously effective and precise — the aeroplane will allegedly do immaculate point-rolls — and hard back pressure on the wheel from fast cruise will have you over the top of a loop before you know it.

And when you finish marvelling at how the Staggerwing flies, there is one last delight. As you select landing gear *down*, there is a chain-over-sprockets rattle, a long-drawn-out clacking like a ship dropping anchor. On it goes until the green *down-and-locked* light blinks on. The novelty of hearing that unusual symphony should always be sufficient reminder to lower the gear for landing, but in the 1930s it was a popular Beech sales pitch to take a prospective buyer for a ride, stop the engine with the propeller horizontal, then land without dropping the wheels. Disaster? No, they just hoisted the strong aeroplane up, extended its legs and flew away. Very reassuring.

To Americans the Staggerwing is *the* antique biplane. In Tullahoma, Tennessee, there is a Staggerwing Museum where you can find examples of many production models. Seven hundred and eighty-one Staggerwings were built, and more than 100 are still flying. Most numerous was the Pratt & Whitney-powered D17S, but you may still find examples of the Jacobs-engined Beeches, so-called 'poor men's Staggerwing', though no Staggerwing owner could ever have been that poor, for the cheapest sold for $12,380 in 1940, and the G17S, the last production model manufactured post-war, was a built-to-order limousine with a $29,000 price tag. A G17S Staggerwing has the same 450 hp engine as the D17S but in an even cleaner airframe, and is the most treasured of all. Only 20 were built before the Bonanza took over as flagship of the Beechcraft line.

Occasionally Staggerwing owners are invited to bring their aeroplanes back to the birthplace at Wichita for a reunion at Beech Field. They come from all over the United States and Canada, lining up the old biplanes on the ramp for Walter Beech's widow Olive Ann to inspect, remembering perhaps when she started work as Beech's secretary at Travel Air in 1925. If she offered the Staggerwing owners a straight trade for any of the shiny new aeroplanes sitting at the factory, I doubt that there would be a single taker, and that is the greatest compliment they could pay her late husband's masterpiece. The Staggerwing, a transport of pure delight.

Staggerwing instrument panel showing the famous 'throwover' control wheel mounted on a central pedestal so that the aircraft can be flown from either seat. Propeller, throttle and mixture controls are mounted vertically down the centre of the panel.

Short Flying Boats

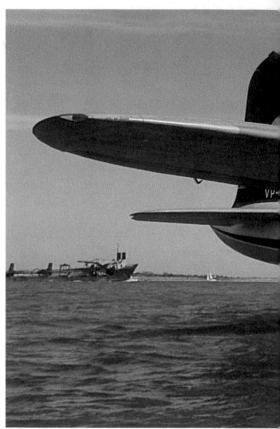

'Hi! Welcome aboard. Have a nice flight'. The standard airline greeting. But there normality ends, for the passenger 'gate' is a pitching motor launch (this is the only airline whose passengers go green *before* take-off), the airport is a stretch of open sea, and the destination: nowhere. We are embarked for a flight in a Short Sandringham, one of the last big four-engined flying boats still airworthy. A nostalgia trip.

No better place for that than here at Calshot, on the south coast of England, where you can stand in the shadow of the derelict castle on the spot where the victorious British Schneider Trophy team posed self-consciously with their Supermarine Racers in 1931, and look across a stretch of water where Short Singapores, Supermarine Southamptons and Blackburn Perths, the Royal Air Force's aerial galleons, rode at anchor in the 1920s and '30s, or sit in the bar of *The Flying Boat* pub, with a former air gunner on Sunderlands telling you how it was his job not only to fight off the Luftwaffe on long maritime patrols but also to cook breakfast, lunch, tea and supper for the 13-man crew on a primus stove. On the sandspit, where sailing boats beat out a rhythm on their wind-whipped rigging, the last two giant Saro Princess flying boats, unwanted behemoths that were the swan-song of the flying boat era, ended their days, cocooned from everything but time. A few miles up Southampton Water, Imperial Airways had a base for their splendid C Class *Empire* boats, which operated long, leisurely services to wherever the map was coloured red. Later, British Overseas Airways kept Boeing Clippers, Sunderlands, Solents and Sandringhams like this one there, and if you were lucky you might spot a visiting Pan American Sikorsky or a French Latécoère. The last flying boats to ply this stretch of water commercially were Aquila Airways'

Short Solents, which ferried tourists in grand style to Madeira before the days of package holidays and jam-packed airliners. The last one left in 1958, to end its days beached like a whale on the banks of the Tagus, made redundant by concrete runways and kerosene-burning jets.

Now *Southern Cross* has returned, brought home after a career in Australia and the Caribbean to become a flying museum piece. She has room for 42 passengers in five separate cabins, four on the lower deck and an upstairs lounge aft of the wing trailing edge. Such luxury! Deep-cushioned blue velour seats facing fore and aft with enough legroom to stretch full length if you wish, down-filled silk cushions, wood-panelling, thick carpets and intimate, subdued lighting. A veritable air-yacht, so sumptuous and untypical of an airliner (a modern one at least) that the seat belts which we fasten seem incongruous and unnecessary. Surely we can just stroll about?

Southern Cross's long-time skipper, and the world's most experienced flying boat captain, is Ron Gillies, with more than 40 years on Sunderlands and Sandringhams. Through the generous picture windows of cabin B we watch a boat scurrying about checking for obstructions on the 'runway'. Driftwood can turn a flying boat into a submarine more

This Short Sandringham flying boat was operated by Antilles Air Boats in the Virgin Islands and has now returned to England where it is to be restored for pleasure flying and aerial cruising.

Imperial Airways *Caledonia* against the familiar Manhattan skyline.

Canopus, most-famous of Imperial Airways' Empire Class Short C flying boats, taking off from the River Medway in Kent, near the Short Brothers factory.

Just coming up 'on the step', an RAF Coastal Command Short Sunderland, affectionately known as 'The Flying Porcupine' to crews in World War II.

A BOAC Short Hythe (civilian conversion of the Sunderland) about to alight in the Solent where (at Hythe, appropriately) BOAC had its flying-boat base in postwar years.

quickly than you would believe, for the skin is not the boiler plate of ships. *All clear!* The mooring is slipped, the forward hatch closed, and number one engine fires up, yawing the boat sharply to starboard until number four catches and we are away — no brakes at sea. As we taxy downwind, Gillies starts the inner pair of Pratt & Whitney R-1830 radial engines and runs through power and propeller checks two engines at a time, then throttles back on three and four to swing the boat around for take-off.

One third flap, up to full power, 2,700 rpm, control column hard back. The rasp of the Pratt & Whitneys penetrates the cabin for an instant before the windows are deluged with water. For long seconds it seems we may have become a submarine, while Gillies juggles throttles, rudder and ailerons to keep *Southern Cross* running straight. Suddenly an invisible hand wipes the windows clear, the thrumming below the deck subsides to a gentle swishing, and we can see the wing floats riding clear of the water. Like a giant powerboat *Southern Cross* is riding the step across the water, accelerating rapidly until at 80 knots, almost one minute into the take-off run, the swishing subsides. Nothing else. No great clawing climb out, no seat-gripping rotation. The metamorphosis from boat to aeroplane is scarcely discernible, and within seconds people are discarding those foolish seatbelts and rushing to the windows as if to convince themselves that this great metal fish really has flown.

Flying off water is a new experience for all of us, and the effect is extra-ordinary. We grin foolishly, and strangers who would never dream of speaking in a railway carriage chat excitedly. One or two even applaud. There is nothing like the novelty of a new (or in this case old) form of transport to break down natural reticence: it is the same on Concorde. But there is no Mach meter clicking off the speed of sound in *Southern Cross's* cabin, nor any Public Address announcement. The captain would sound a little foolish explaining that we will be cruising at 125 knots and that our altitude will be less than 500 feet. The low-level flight is not just a concession to our short-duration flight. Flying boat travel was ever thus, low and leisurely, with time to enjoy a fine cigar in the smoking room and gaze out at the pyramids as you flew low along the Nile, or at the herds of wild animals as you made your way along the African coast. One Imperial Airways flying boat captain lost his cap through an open cock-pit window and swears that on his next trip he saw it on the head of an elephant!

We make a gentle sweep round towards the Isle of Wight. Ron Gillies invites interested passengers to visit the flight deck, as any good flying boat skipper would. A mistake. *Everyone* wants to go aloft, and they all surge forwards in a rush which has the crew winding on great handfuls of nose-up trim in the cockpit. When there are nine people up there they tactfully suggest, *perhaps three at a time?* Space is no problem. There is room for a dozen or more on the fight deck (or should that be bridge?), but the working end of the boat contrasts starkly with the plush comfort below. The seats are of battered and worn leather, and the size and style of the instruments reflect the aeroplane's age and military origins, with huge control wheels eminently suitable for a maritime craft. And although *Southern Cross* is equipped with modern navigational aids there are reminders of her special role in the racks of flares, a drift sight, an astrodrome for taking star shots, and a curtained-off navigator's plotting table.

The sun has been down half an hour, and from the astrodome the first stars are faintly visible. Along the top of the wing blue-violet flames from the Pratt & Whitneys lick out at the the purple dusk. It is a rare and moving sight, riding the back of an ancient sea bird and gazing out across an ocean. Well, it may only be the English Channel, but a man can dream, can't he? I am reminded of a dream the great helicopter and flying boat pioneer Igor Sikorsky had as a boy in Tsarist Russia. 'I saw myself walking along a narrow, luxuriously decorated passage-way,' he wrote in his autobiography. 'On both sides were walnut doors, similar to the staterooms in a steamer. The floor was covered with an attractive carpet. A spherical electric light from the ceiling produced a pleasant bluish illumination. Walking slowly I felt a slight vibration under my feet and was not surprised to find that the feeling was different from that experienced on a steamer or railway train, because I knew I was on board a large flying ship in the air'.

That was in 1900. Thirty-one years later Sikorsky's dream came true when he rode aboard his S-40 *American Clipper* over New York at dusk. I can guess how he felt: there is a dream-like quality about a craft which combines the relaxed luxury of an ocean liner with the sensation of flight.

Throttled back to 2,000 rpm and 20 inches of manifold pressure, *Southern*

Another view of the
Sandringham *Southern Cross*.

The last civilian flying boat
built by Short Brothers was
the Solent. This BOAC Solent
is seen in the Pool of London
after passing beneath London
Bridge.

Cross cruises the shores of the Isle of Wight so low that we can read the neon signs on the pubs and nightclubs, wingtips level with the clifftops. A man walking his terrier on the sands looks up and waves as we roar above him. We all wave back.

Southern Cross makes a sweeping turn around the Needles rocks, silhouetted in the afterglow, then heads back past Queen Victoria's residence at Osborne House, and on past the Royal Yacht Squadron at Cowes, turning towards the invisible water runway. One-third flap, airspeed 115 knots, power up to 2,500 rpm, airspeed back to 100 knots, two-thirds flap, setting up a classic flying boat approach at a constant rate of descent in near level attitude until she touches the water at 75 knots, our arrival marked only by the gentle hiss from the keel. But as she decelerates and the keel bites deeper and the lift goes from her wings the water hammers below like a pneumatic drill, louder and louder until, with a roar, the boat rears nose-up and comes off the step, throwing a deluge of water and spray over the cabin windows as she settles. We are a boat again.

Taxying on the water requires the skills of a boatman rather than those of a pilot. There is no stopping of course, and steering is accomplished by use of differential throttle, aileron and rudder. In calm conditions the outer engines alone provide adequate steering, but in strong winds the flying boat's tendency to weathercock into wind demands some slick co-ordination of throttle levers, control column and rudder pedals, and a keen sense of anticipation to keep her pointed in the right direction.

This evening it is calm. Ron Gillies turns on the landing lights and brings up the power again on one and four until *Southern Cross* is fast-taxying on the step, planing across the water with tip floats and silvery propeller arcs brilliantly illuminated, shards of backlit spray darting incandescent into the night. We rumble slowly up to the mooring buoy, engines shut down, as a crewman leans from the forward hatch with a boathook to catch the line and tie up.

'That was some flight,' one of the passengers observes as we board the launch again. He is wrong. We have not flown at all. We have voyaged.

Piper J3 Cub

Yellow is the colour of my true love's hair, went the old song, and if you learned to fly in America in the forties or early fifties chances are that it was also the colour of the aeroplane nearest your heart. Like Henry Ford's all-black Model Ts, William T. Piper's Cub came in any colour you wanted as long as it was yellow. *Sport Yellow* they called it, with a black lightning flash along the fuselage and a smiling brown teddy bear motif on the fin.

The Cub's name originated from an otherwise forgettable aero engine called the Brownbach Tiger Kitten. But let us go back for a moment to the year 1926. C. Gilbert Taylor and Gordon Taylor were two self-taught aircraft engineers from Rochester, New York who marketed a two-seat, parasol-wing monoplane called Chummy. It did not sell, and when Gordon died two years later C. G. Taylor moved off to Bradford, Pennsylvania,

where the good citizens invested some $50,000 in the Taylor Brothers Aircraft Corporation. Among the backers was a wealthy oilman, William T. Piper, who knew nothing about aeroplanes but had a shrewd business sense. He was quick to see that at $4,000 the Chummy had little chance in those depressed times. What the country needed, aside from the proverbial five-cent cigar, was a cheap little lightplane. Taylor designed him one, the E-2, and since its 20 hp engine was a Tiger Kitten, what better name for the aircraft than Cub?

Alas, a cute name did not prevent the company going bankrupt. In 1931 Piper acquired the liquidated firm for just $761, retained Taylor as president and chief engineer, and ordered a batch of 37 hp engines from Continental Motors. The union of the Continental with the E-2 was successful, although the Piper/Taylor marriage was not — Taylor left in 1936 to set up his rival Taylorcraft firm after a string of policy disagreements with Piper, who had hired a young New Jersey engineer named Walter Jamouneau to improve the company's designs. 'Feel free to make any changes in the design of the E-2 when Taylor isn't around,' Piper told him. Jamouneau's refinements resulted in the 1936 Taylor J-2 Cub, which had a 37 hp Continental A-40 engine and immediately became the 'flivver of the air' that Piper had been seeking. The Bradford production line turned J-2 Cubs out at the rate of 20 each week. Piper piled them high and sold them cheap — $1,270 or $425 down and the rest by monthly instalments — and employed a battalion of

This Cub is identified as a former military L-4 'Grasshopper' observation aircraft by the extended 'glasshouse' cabin.

salesmen to tour the country in Cubs. He offered them an extra dollar on their expenses for every night spent in a different place, and $25 for every sale made on the spot (they had to remember to collect an extra $10 from the buyer for the compass, which was not part of the deal, or remove it before parting with the aeroplane).

Business burgeoned thanks to salesmen whom Piper reckoned worked better 'if they're kept a mite hungry'. Five hundred and fifteen J-2 Cubs were sold in the first year. Then, one night in March 1937, the Bradford factory was razed to the ground by a fire fuelled with wood, aircraft dope and gasoline. It was the end of the Taylor Aircraft Company, but the beginning of the Piper Aircraft Corporation, for Piper's response to this calamity was to set up shop again in a disused silk mill at nearby Lock Haven,

right alongside the local airfield. He doubled the workforce, renamed the company and offered The New Cub at a bargain price of $995.

This was the archetypal J-3 Cub, which was to become so familiar to the hundreds of thousands of Americans who had their aerial baptisms in it that the name fell into common use as a generic term for any aircraft smaller than a DC-3. You will still hear people talking about 'these little Piper Cubs' as they board sophisticated $150,000 lightplanes today.

The New Cub was offered with a choice of 40 hp, 50 hp, 55 hp and 65 hp engines, but the J-3C/65 with a 65 hp Continental A-65 powerplant proved most popular. Piper's salesmanship was truly astonishing. Before long he had a worldwide network of 1,500 dealers and a mile-long production line which churned out a gleaming yellow Cub once every 70 minutes. *Count the Cubs* became a Piper slogan. It was difficult not to. At a Miami airshow, 261 out of 625 aircraft attending were Cubs. Ten cents bought you a little Cub bear emblem on a stick-pin. A tobacco company gave away a Cub on its radio show every week for a year and a half. In 1941 48 Cubs, one for every State of the Union, toured the country emblazoned with Royal Air Force roundels and the name *Flitfire,* drumming up funds for the RAF Benevolent Fund in Britain with the aid of 48 winsome young ladies who rode in their back seats.

The Cub is a classic lightplane design, instantly familiar to any youngster who ever built a model aircraft: high wing,

More than 1,000 L-4 Grasshoppers of the U.S. Army took part in the Allied invasion of Europe in 1944. This restored example carries the identifying black-and-white D-Day stripes applied to British and American aircraft supporting the landings.

Green grass, yellow Cub: a
Piper J-3C/65 is a fine flying
machine for a summer's day.

slabsided fuselage, fat doughnut tyres on
an undercarriage set well forward. Model
Cubs make fine performers. Its structure
is simplicity itself: welded steel fuselage,
wood-and-aluminium or, more commonly,
all-aluminium wings with fabric covering. There is not even a proper fuel gauge,
just a cork float with wire-rod level
indicator which projects through the filler
cap in front of the windscreen. The cork
sometimes becomes saturated and loses
buoyancy, so a visual check of fuel
contents should be an essential part of
preflight inspection. As the indicator is

ungraduated, accurate inflight assessment of fuel state is an acquired art.

Climbing into a Cub through its horizontally split door means jack-knifing,
backing in and twisting around while
swinging a leg over the control column
and keeping your feet off the wing struts.
A practised limbo dancer will find it easy.
Others will likely find themselves facing
the wrong way with a leg left dangling
outside at first try. Flying controls are
duplicated, but there is only one set of
instruments, up front. If flown solo the
pilot must occupy the rear seat to keep

icing. Not relishing the prospect of a forced landing and a long or possibly permanent sojourn in the frozen wastes, the pilot had his passenger glide the Cub in a level attitude whilst he climbed onto the undercarriage and pulled the propeller through until the engine fired again. A young woman pilot is said to have done the same while flying solo over the North Sea.

Visibility is typical for a high-wing tailwheel aircraft: rather poor, especially from the back seat, so ground manoeuvring requires constant side-to-side weaving. Leaving the cabin doors open helps, since one can then lean out to see ahead. Take-off (no flaps, the Cub does not have them) is brisk, breaking ground at about 38 mph. With a moderate headwind 50 yards ground run is all that a Cub needs. Elevator trimming is accomplished by a screw-jack which adjusts the incidence of the tailplane, quite an innovation in its day. The cabin is noisy at the Cub's leisurely maximum cruise speed of 90 mph, with a barrage of sound from engine, slipstream and airframe vibration which is wearing on a long trip, but then a Cub's economic cruise speed of around 70 mph makes it no aeroplane for dashing hither and yon. If you are battling against a headwind cars will be going faster. And in any case, although the Cub will go about 220 miles on a full

This J-3C/65 Cub is owned by a British airline pilot and pictured over Buckinghamshire.

within the aeroplane's centre of gravity range.

A standard J-3 Cub has no electrics and must be hand-propped for starting. Piper sales brochures made much of the machine's single-handed operational capability, pointing out that by standing behind the engine it was possible to reach the throttle and swing the propeller yourself — a practice which resulted in many a pilotless take-off but proved useful in emergencies. Two trappers on a hunting trip in northern Canada suffered an engine stoppage through carburettor

tank, the rudimentary seats do not encourage marathon journeys. Seats on
early Cubs were even more rudimentary
until the day William T. himself ferried
one from Pennsylvania to California . . .

But for those prepared to make their
progress at a stately pace, with frequent
stops, a Cub is a splendidly unhurried
way to travel. It is so inherently stable
that it will fly hands-off indefinitely
whilst you nibble a sandwich or consult a
chart. A Cub is a natural platform for
eyeball navigation. A friend of mine used
to find his way around by cruising along
at 500 feet with the door open while his
wife read road signs through binoculars.
And if you do get lost, the Cub's impecc-
able low-speed handling and amazing
short-field performance turns any farmer's

field into an airport. Small wonder that
during World War II the U.S. Army ordered nearly 6,000 J-3s for observation and
artillery spotting duties. Army Cubs were
called L-4s, or more popularly Grasshoppers, allegedly because a crusty old
cavalry brigade commander remarked to
a civilian pilot taking part in the 1941
Third Army Manoeuvres at El Paso, Texas,
that his J-3 had 'looked just like a goddam
grasshopper out there in the boondocks'.
A Cub was certainly the aeroplane for
dodging the cactus. Grasshoppers served
in all major theatres of war right up to
Korea. During the invasion of Sicily, L-4s
flew off platforms mounted atop tank
landing craft. At Okinawa they were
hoisted aloft from a cable strung between
stanchions on landing ships. A bazooka-
equipped Cub knocked out five German
tanks during the Battle of the Bulge. One
thousand went to France in support of the
Allied invasion in 1944, operating in
forward areas from fields and roads. Even
comedian Bob Hope was moved to include
the J-3 among his wisecracks for the
troops. 'A Cub', he said, 'is a P-51 that
wouldn't eat its cereal.'

I doubt that there is any part of this
globe in which Cubs have not flown.
From pastures, dirt strips, lakes, roads,
glaciers, paddy fields, carrier decks, even
from special platforms on cars, trucks and
trains. Cubs have alighted on endless
combinations of wheels, bogies, floats,
skis, hydrofoils and even caterpillar
tracks. One was experimentally fitted
with inflatable rubber floats. Their
inventor thought they would overcome
the problem of flotsam damage which
imperilled metal-floated aircraft. They
did. But when the rubber-shod pneumatic
Cub climbed to altitude, the lower air

pressure caused the floats to inflate like balloons, with a disastrous effect on the Cub's already slow progress.

There have been low-wing Cubs, mid-wing Cubs, biplane Cubs, Cubs with all manner of strange engines, even a Cub with no engine at all — the Piper TG-8 glider trainer in which unfortunate GIs who had not qualified for conventional flight training were given (very) basic flying instruction before being sent off to pilot overladen troop-carrying gliders into the battlefields of Europe. There was a Cub Composite — two Cubs mounted pick-a-back by an airshow performer, and a Siamese Cub which comprised two J-3s joined side-by-side like North American's F-82 Twin Mustang. Why? I cannot say, but despite rumours from their rivals it was not Piper's way of wooing potential Cub customers who sought the safety of two engines. No aeroplane has been so used and abused as the Cub.

Piper built 14,125 J-3 Cubs, including the L-4 Grasshoppers for the Putt-Putt Air Force. For the best part of three decades more student pilots learned their craft in Cubs than in any other kind of aeroplane, and learned to love them for their viceless (but not easy) handling, honest, gentle performance and the sheer challenge of trying to make a perfect bounce-free landing on those low-pressure doughnuts of tyres. But the story did not end with Cub No. 14,125. Forty-thousand Cubs and Cub derivatives have been built, for the ageless J-3 has sired generations of derivatives. One, the Piper PA-18 Super Cub, is still in production in 1981. It has a 150 hp engine, flaps, and 40 years of refinement, but it is still unmistakably a Cub. Piper do not feature this rag-winged throwback from a bygone age in their glossy advertising, but the Lock Haven factory still builds them for farmers, bush-fliers and nostalgic private owners who have found nothing better in half a century's flying. One thing has changed, though. A Sport Yellow colour scheme for a 1980s Super Cub costs an extra $995 — the same price as a complete J-3 cost back in 1940.

Entry into the Cub's cabin requires practice, but the horizontally divided door provides excellent ventilation on the ground or in the air and makes the aircraft ideal for aerial photography.

Douglas DC-3

'I don't think much of this, Bill, do you?' Cyrus Rowlett Smith remarked to his companion as they lurched and bounced through ice and turbulence between Buffalo and Chicago one day in 1934. Smith was president of American Airlines. Bill Littlewood was his chief engineer. The aeroplane was a Douglas DC-2 twin-engine transport with which American was forging a network of transcontinental routes which would make it the largest airline in the United States. The DC-2 was a fine aeroplane, fast, yet costing no more to operate than a Ford Tri Motor. But it had shortcomings. The narrow 14-passenger cabin was cramped, payload was limited, and it lacked the range to fly the popular New York-Chicago route nonstop. And as Smith's stomach was discovering, it was directionally unstable in rough air.

Smith's philosophy of airline management was simple: give passengers a fast, safe and comfortable ride at a sensible price. His airline's old Curtiss Condor biplanes, the Flying Brooklyn Bridges, had sleeping bunks in which passengers could slumber their way across America. Why not a sleeper version of the DC-2? In American's battle for passengers against

The ageless 'Dizzy Three' still earns its keep the world over nearly half a century after it first appeared. This colourful example is operating in Colombia.

United and TWA it would be a major selling point. Smith telephoned Donald Douglas as soon as he reached Chicago. Could he build him a sleeper DC-3 with a wider cabin to accommodate pullman-sized bunks, new 1,000 hp Wright Cyclone R-1820-G engines in place of the DC-2's 750 hp Cyclones to increase the payload, and greater range to enable the aircraft to traverse the nation in four hops and reach Chicago from the East Coast in one jump? Douglas demurred. His factory was fully stretched on DC-2 production. Smith persisted, in a long-distance call which lasted two hours. He promised an order for such an aircraft sight unseen. Finally Douglas agreed to a design study for a Douglas Sleeper Transport. On 8 July 1935 Smith cabled Douglas: 'Enter our order for ten DST airplanes.' The price was $79,500 each. 'Even if they buy 20 of our ships we'll be lucky to break even,' Douglas complained. He did better. When the last of the DST derivatives came off the production line in May 1946, Douglas's company had built 10,656 and grossed more than one billion dollars on sales.

The first DST flew from Clover Field, Santa Monica, California on 17 December 1935 — 32 years to the day from the Wright Brothers' first flight. Dubbed DST

Sky Sleeper, it had sleeping accommodation for 12 passengers in the main cabin and another two in a special private Sky Room (popularly known as the Honeymoon Hut) immediately behind the cockpit. In Day configuration it could carry 21 passengers and was known as the DC-3 Dayplane.

The DST entered service on the New York-Chicago route on 25 June 1936, with a scheduled time en route of four hours forty-five minutes westbound and three hours fifty-five minutes eastbound, compared to a railway journey of 18 hours. Three months later American launched

above
In military guise the DC-3 became the C-47, beloved Gooney Bird of the USAAF. This one, in typical take-off attitude, is part of the Confederate Air Force collection and carries D-Day invasion stripes over its olive-drab camouflage.

the 'Mercury' coast-to-coast service which flew from Newark, New Jersey to Grand Central Air Terminal at Glendale, California with stops at Memphis, Dallas and Tucson. In less than six months of operation the new Douglases turned American's loss of $2.3 million in 1934 to a small profit of $4,590 in 1936. Other airlines soon found their fortunes similarly changed by the DC-3, which was the first airliner whose combination of payload, range and operational costs enabled profits to be made solely from the carriage of passengers, without need of government airmail subsidies.

Such was the total dominance of the DC-3 that by December 1937 production was running at 36 aircraft per month to meet demand from U.S. and overseas customers. Two years later hardly any other type was in use by major airlines in the United States, and nine out of ten airline services worldwide were operated by the Douglas. When America entered World War II in December 1941 507 DC-3s had been delivered, but that was but a tiny foretaste of what was to come. In military guise, as the C-47, C-53, C-117 and R4D, another 9,825 were manufactured at Santa Monica, Long Beach and Oklahoma City factories, reaching a peak output of 4,878 aircraft in 1944. The DC-3 in various forms was almost certainly the only aircraft type to serve all major combatants in World War II. The British and American forces used them in vast numbers; the Japanese and Russians were manufacturing DC-3s under licence

before hostilities began; and the Luftwaffe pressed into service a collection of Douglases impounded from civil operators as the Nazis overran Europe. During the Allied invasion of France in June 1944 more than 1,000 C-47s ferried troops across the English Channel, carrying unbelievable overloads. The aeroplane which began as a 21-passenger airliner routinely hauled 50, 60, 70, once even *98* people. If it would fit inside (or even if it would not) the DC-3 would carry it. The trick, one former crewman friend of mine recalls, was to 'shove everything as far forward as it would go,' and if that was not enough you might even have to wind on full nose-down trim just to raise the tail for take-off.

DST, DC-3, Douglas Racer, C-47, Gooney Bird, Dakota, Dizzy-Three, Skytrain, call it what you will, the DC-3 became the most successful transport aircraft ever built, perhaps ever likely to be. When the war ended surplus DC-3s formed the nucleus of airline fleets around the world, selling for bargain prices of little more than $1,000 apiece. Douglas produced a final batch of civilian DC-3s from military C-117 components before finally closing down the production line in May 1946 after a ten year run. In 1948 nearly 2,000 DC-3s were in commercial service. Perhaps half that number are flying yet, and some 400 are still carrying fare-paying passengers and commercial cargo. There have been countless attempts to produce the ideal DC-3 replacement. Few have matched the

Who could fail to recognize that profile? Atmospheric 1930s shot of a DC-3 at Washington National Airport.

I am the captain, I sit on the left . . . A battered and worn confusion of knobs, levers, taps and handles that has been home to countless thousands of pilots for nearly half a century.

Douglas for its 'can-do' ability to haul impossible loads from improbable places in safety and at low cost. The only DC-3 replacement is another DC-3, say purists, and they may be right.

Certainly one rarely meets anyone who has earned his living up in the beak of this ancient bird whose eyes do not moisten at the memory of the DC-3's cockpit, smelling of old leather, metal, hydraulic fluid, oil, petrol, cigarette smoke, the sweat of a hundred palms and the lingering tang of a thousand cargoes. It bears the well-worn patina of tens of thousands of flying hours and maybe millions of miles of travel across the earth, of which I will wager that there is not one square mile on which a DC-3's wings have not cast their distinctive shadow, or which has not echoed the rumble of a pair of Pratt & Whitney engines. *Trust in God and Pratt & Whitney* went the old prayer of Dizzy-Three crews, and rarely indeed did the Pratts not respond to your trust, God was not always so co-operative,

though. Nor were the Wright Cyclone engines installed in some DC-3s. Pilot lore has it that the Wrights vibrated more than the Pratts, and it was said that American Airlines' pilots (AA had Wright-engined DSTs and DC-3s) were noted for the number of visits they made to the aeroplanes' aft lavatories to relieve their throbbing kidneys.

On the pre-war routes it was usually the co-pilot's job to mingle with the passengers during a flight to answer their questions and circulate his captain's report (signed by both crew members) of airspeed, altitude and destination weather. Very official. No little jingles and *This is your captain speaking* over public address systems then. And a captain ran a tight ship. *He* flew the aeroplane, while the co-pilot performed such menial tasks as befitted his lowly status and the captain would entrust to him: filling in the airmail forms and flight logs, retracting the flaps and undercarriage, fine-tuning the mixture and propeller controls, and working the radio. Just occasionally a captain might give his apprentice the chance to do the take-off or make a landing, but the chain of command was strict and sacrosanct, and the best co-pilot was one who knew how to do as he was told. This verse, penned in the early 1940s by Colonial (now Eastern) Airlines' Keith Murray, captures the finely-balanced cockpit relationship perfectly:

I am the Captain, I sit on the left,
I'm very skilful and terribly deft.
I suffer in silence while Joe on my right
Makes all his circuits a little too tight.
I never go crook when he drops too much flap;
I like his sweet smile as he says 'Sorry, Cap!'
Then bashes the trim with a twist and a twirl,
As he raves of the virtues and curves of his girl.
I select cruising power and call for coarse pitch,
Joe grabs the mixtures and slams it to Rich.
When it's time to change tanks Joe turns the wrong tap,
When I call for gear up he drops ten degrees flap.
He's late for take-off first flight each morning,
I do the run-up while Joe does the yawning.
He's never quite sure of his check-points or courses,
I fake the log while Joe swots the horses.
When I give him a landing he gives me the pip
As the tower calls up and says 'Stay on the strip!',
'Ignorant type,' says Joe on my right;
Then dates up the hostess for Saturday night.

When the ceiling's right down and I fly on the gauges,
Joe says a prayer and chants Rock of Ages.
I envy the guy who said God is my Co,
Oh, what I'd give to swap him for Joe!

While from the other side of the cockpit:

I am the co-pilot I sit on the right
It's up to me to be quick and bright;
I never talk back for I have regrets,
But I have to remember what the captain forgets.
I make out the flight plan and study the weather,
Pull up the gear, and standby to feather;
Make out the mail form and do the reporting,
And fly the old crate while the captain is courting.
I take the readings, adjust the power
Put on the heaters, when we're in a shower;
Tell where we are on the darkest night,
And do all the bookwork without any light.
I call for the captain and buy him Cokes;
I always laugh at his corny jokes,
And once in a while when his landings are rusty,
I always come through with 'By gosh, but it's gusty!'
All in all I'm a general stooge,
As I sit on the right of the man they call Scrooge;
I guess you think that it's past understanding,
But maybe someday he'll give me a landing?

Given the chance, young Joe on the right would have found the DC-3 easy enough to fly. It had inherent stability and was forgiving of even the worst all-thumbs co-pilot. For instrument flying the DC-3 provided a steady platform with

Pratts rumbling, brakes squealing, ancient bones creaking, a DC-3 sets out on another flight, still earning a living in the age of supersonic transport.

Kicking up the dust. A DC-3 is happy on tarmac or grass and will haul all that will fit into it into any airfield worthy of the name, and many that are not. This pristine example is owned by an American college.

none of the directional hunting of its predecessor, and a low stalling speed, combined with excellent control response at low airspeed, gave it fine short-field performance. A practised DC-3 pilot could slip into just about any airfield worthy of the name and a great many that were not, and could get out again on the lift of that elegant, swept-back wing and the combined 2,400 hp of the two Pratt & Whitneys. One C-47 was flown out of a tiny jungle strip in the Pacific carrying an entire wing from another Gooney Bird slung beneath its fuselage. Another DC-3 belonging to China National Airways Corporation flew not on the proverbial wing and prayer but on a wing-and-a-bit: its starboard wing panel, damaged by Japanese gunfire, was replaced by a DC-2 wing some five feet shorter, making it a hybrid 'DC-2½'. It flew. Indeed, so efficient was the DC-3's classic wing design

that the U.S. Army successfully tested an engineless glider C-47 called the XCG-17, and some C-47s with combat-damaged engines were air-towed back to repair bases.

If you travel much by air around the world, chances are that some day, somewhere, you may still find yourself holding a ticket for a journey in a DC-3. You may find it cramped and claustrophobic compared to modern jets. You will certainly find it noisier. But I defy you not to be moved by this splendid aeroplane, perhaps the world's most successful flying machine, which brought prosperity to the airlines and has done as much as any vehicle known to man to open up the remotest, obscurest corners of the world. And when its 50th anniversary comes up in 1985 you may be certain that the DC-3 will still be earning someone a living.

below
Not all DC-3s have 'trusted in God and Pratt & Whitney'. This is one of two modified to test Rolls-Royce Dart turboprop engines for British European Airways prior to the introduction of the Vickers Viscount airliner, and was known as the 'Dart Dakota'. A three-engine turbine conversion (the third engine installed in the nose) has recently been made in the United States.

BEA EXPRESS AIR FREIGHT
G-AMDB
BRITISH EUROPEAN AIRWAYS

Messerschmitt Bf109E

While Jesse Owens, the 'Ebony Antelope' was winning the adulation of the crowds and four gold medals at the Olympic Games in Berlin in 1936, another lithe, fast-moving newcomer made its debut over the Olympic Stadium. It was a single-seat fighter aeroplane whose name was to become synonymous with Nazi air power — the Messerschmitt Bf109.

That Willi Messerschmitt's Bayerische Flugzeugwerke AG (BFW) should have been afforded such prominence at the XI Olympiad was as extraordinary as Jesse Owens' performance, for Messerschmitt had fallen foul of Erhard Milch, then a director of the German airline Lufthansa, in 1928, and when the influential Milch became Minister of Aviation at the Reichsluftfahrtministerium he saw to it that BFW received no official contracts or development finance for its designs. Adding insult to injury, he went so far as to order Messerschmitt to build designs of his arch-rival Ernst Heinkel under licence. In 1933, with bankruptcy looming, Messerschmitt and his co-director Rakan Kokothaki contracted to design a new airliner for Romania. Milch was furious. Why, he demanded, was Professor Messerschmitt producing aeroplanes for foreign countries when the Fatherland was rapidly expanding its own military and civil aviation programmes? Messerschmitt pointed out that he had been forced to solicit orders elsewhere because of Milch's own vindictive policies. As a result the RLM gave BFW an order to develop a touring aircraft for the 4th *Challenge de Tourisme Internationale* of 1934, and invited Messerschmitt to compete with Arado, Focke-Wulf and Heinkel in the design of a new fighter. Milch felt confident that Messerschmitt's design would fail to measure up to requirements and that he would thus be discredited. And even if his design won the competition there would be no guarantee of a production order.

opposite
That narrow-track undercarriage resulted in five percent of the 35,000-plus Messerschmitt Bf109s built being written off in landing accidents. This Bf109E-3 is preserved at the Royal Air Force Museum, Hendon, near London.

This Messerschmitt Bf109E-3B is part of the Royal Air Force Museum's Battle of Britain collection housed at Hendon, near London.

below

A Messerschmitt Bf109E-4/Trop (Tropical version) operating with JG 27 in North Africa, photographed in September 1941. The poor cockpit visibility is evident in this shot.

Messerschmitt decided to gamble. He began work on a most advanced concept making use of every modern technique: all-metal monocoque construction, cantilever wings with flaps and automatic slots, retractable landing gear, fully enclosed cockpit, and the most powerful engine then available in Germany — the Junkers Jumo 210A 610 hp liquid-cooled V-12. However, the Jumo was not ready when Messerschmitt's first airframe was, so ironically the prototype Messerschmitt Bf109V1 was powered by a British Rolls-Royce Kestrel, forerunner of the Merlin which was to power the 109's principal adversaries, Hurricane and Spitfire.

This prototype made its first flight from BFW's Augsburg airfield in September 1935, flown by test pilot Flugkapitän 'Bubi' Knötsch, who later ferried it to the Luftwaffe test centre at Berlin-Rechlin, where its narrow-track landing gear collapsed on arrival. It was a portent of things to come, because the narrow gear, which placed the weight of the aircraft on

the fuselage rather than on Messerschmitt's light, non-too-strong wings, made the aeroplane wallow badly on the rough grass airfields of the day, and caused it to swing on take-off and ground-loop on landing. This remained a weakness throughout the 109's long career. Perhaps five percent of the 35,000-plus aircraft built were written off in ground handling accidents. General Ernst Udet once remarked to Willi Messerschmitt: 'One thing, dear Messerschmitt, must be made clear between us. There must be no more aircraft lost in normal landings as a result of faulty under-carriages: this can hardly be described as a technical novelty in aircraft construction.'

The repaired Bf 109V1 and the Heinkel He 112 emerged as clear favourites in the opening round of the fighter competition held at the Luftwaffe test centre at Travemünde in October 1935. In January of the following year the Jumo-engined second prototype (the Olympics aeroplane) joined the programme. This Bf 109V2 had provision for two 7.9mm Rheinmetall MG 17 machine guns mounted atop the engine cowling. When the final fly-off competition took place in the fall of 1936, test pilot Hermann Wurster spun the Bf 109V2 down from 16,000 feet, making 38 turns in all, left and right, then put the fighter in a terminal velocity dive from 24,000 feet which ended near ground level. This demonstration was not emulated by the rival Heinkel. The simpler, out-performing Messerschmitt design won the day; the Reichsluftfahrtministerium decreed that the Bf 109 would be the Luftwaffe's standard fighter aeroplane and the German press began eulogizing the new aircraft. The expansion of Adolf Hitler's aircraft programme and the build-up of the hitherto clandestine Luftwaffe were no longer secrets.

Early production Bf 109s and Cs cut their combat teeth in Spain during the Civil War, but the first mass-production version was the Bf 109E, the 'Emil' (Willi Messerschmitt's second name) which first flew in prototype form in the summer of 1938. This aeroplane differed from earlier variants in having a 1,175 hp fuel-injected Daimler-Benz DB 601A engine. Production Bf 109E-1s began rolling from the now-renamed Messerschmitt AG factory early in 1939, and by the end of that year Messerschmitt and its sub-contractors had built 1,540 Bf 109Es.

The Emil was an advanced fighter for its time. Small and light, it had an initial climb rate of 3,000 feet per minute and a maximum level speed of 354 mph at 12,000 feet — slower than the Spitfire despite having more power. But most important to the Luftwaffe was the fact that the aircraft was readily available, whereas the service entry of both the Hurricane and Spitfire into the Royal Air Force had been subject to protracted delays. By the time war broke out in Europe in September 1939 the Luftwaffe had 1,085 Bf 109s. Towards the end of 1939 the definitive Bf 109E-3 sub-type was in production. This Emil, numerically the most important of all, had an uprated DB 601A engine and five guns — two nose-mounted MG 17s, two wing-mounted Mauser 20mm MG FF cannons and a single cannon firing through the propeller hub. This latter weapon was of dubious value. When fired it produced severe vibrations, and it was rarely employed in combat. Early in 1940, production of E-3s was running at 150 per month, with total production for the year reaching 1,868 aircraft, including export orders from Bulgaria, Hungary, Japan, Romania, Russia, Slovakia, Switzerland and Yugoslavia.

Apart from 15 Bf 109E-1s sent belatedly to the homeward-bound Legion Kondor in Spain in the last days of the spring of 1939, the Emil first saw action when Hitler ordered the invasion of Poland on 1 September. The Bf 109s soon tore the Polish Air Force resistance to pieces in a campaign which lasted a scant 18 days. Such was their total dominance of the air that lumbering Junkers JU-52/3m tri-motor transports were able to overfly the Polish capital Warsaw with impunity, and the brief action afforded the Luftwaffe's Jagdflieger little opportunity to assess their own skills.

Three months later, on 18 December 1939, Bf 109E-3s from III Gruppe Jagdge-schwader 77 attacked a formation of RAF Wellington bombers raiding the port of Wilhelmshaven and shot down half the 24-bomber formation for the loss of two Emils. Thirty Messerschmitts of I Gruppe JG 77 took part in the invasion of Norway which began on 8 April 1940, but again encountered little serious opposition there, or in the Blitzkrieg across the Low Countries, where the Emils were an unequal match for the gallant Dutch in their Fokker D. XXIs, many of which never got off the ground. Thirteen days after Holland capitulated, Belgium also fell. 'The Belgians', observed Major Adolf Galland, fourth highest-scoring Luftwaffe ace of World War II, 'flew antiquated Hurricanes in which even more experienced pilots could have done little against our new Bf 109E. We outstripped them in speed, rate of climb, armament, and above all, in flying experience and training.' Much the same thing happened in France, where the Armée de l'Air's motley collection of fighters were no match for the Emils. Nor were the Gloster Gladiator biplanes of the RAF's British Expeditionary Force Air Contingent. Its Hurricanes fared little better, but pilot inexperience was the decisive factor which left 75 Hurricanes destroyed and a further 120 abandoned when the British pulled out at Dunkirk.

Small wonder then that Reichsmarschall Hermann Göring was confident of his Luftwaffe's ability to deal summarily with the RAF when it began attacking England in the summer of 1940. From July, formations of Emils, Junkers JU-87 Stukas and Messerschmitt Me 110s roamed the English Channel looking for shipping targets and providing both the

Professor Willi Messerschmitt.

Note the outward-retracting undercarriage and strut-braced tailplane in this fine underside view of an *Emil*.

Luftwaffe pilots and the British radar network with some practice for the massive assault which led up to Adler Tag (Eagle Day) on 13 August 1940. The Battle of Britain (though no-one realized it was that at the time) was under way, a battle which the Bf 109, superior in performance, numbers and pilot experience to the bulk of the RAF opposition, should have won decisively. But no. For three weeks Göring's 'young eagles' concentrated their attacks on RAF airfields in the south of England, hell-bent on destroying Fighter Command completely. Despite overwhelming odds the British fliers succeeded in swinging the advantage away from the invaders . . . but only just. When the Luftwaffe's assault was switched away from the airfields to the City of London on 7 September 1940 (largely as a result of Hitler's desire to avenge RAF bombing raids on Berlin), Fighter Command was reeling from incessant attacks, and plans had been laid to move fighter airfields to the north of the British capital, out of range of the Bf 109E escort fighters.

The switch to London, whose citizens took an almost intolerable beating night after night, gave Fighter Command a chance to regroup and make good losses which, unlike the Luftwaffe, they could ill-afford. All the while Hitler's opportunity for invasion was slipping away as the Führer waited for his air force to win mastery of the skies, a victory which never came. Hard-pressed Emil pilots found themselves increasingly unable to protect the bombers to an acceptable degree because of severe range limitations which prevented them from engaging in protracted combat, and the raids diminished.

Which was the better fighter, the Spitfire or the Bf 109E? That question will

never be answered to everyone's satisfaction. Such considerations depend on too many factors for a straigtforward assessment: whether the aircraft in question were new, on peak performance, or old and tired. What was the experience level of each pilot? How many duty hours had he flown that day? Are we talking about high-altitude combat or a low-level running fight? Officially the Spitfire 1A, in service during the Battle of Britain, was faster than the Emil by some 10 mph, with a maximum level speed of 365 mph, but many surviving Luftwaffe pilots, including Adolf Galland, insist that the Messerschmitt had a 10-15 mph advantage.

What was the Messerschmitt like to fly? It was a small machine with a tiny cockpit, cramped for a tall pilot. Sitting in the cockpit of a surviving Emil at the RAF Battle of Britain Museum at Hendon, near London, you can appreciate how a six-footer would have spent most of his time with the top of his flying helmet jammed tight against the roof of the greenhouse canopy. And there was another problem. The fussily-framed canopy afforded dismal pilot visibilty both on the ground and in the air, and since it was hinged sideways it was not possible to open it to improve the outlook in an airfield circuit or on landing approach, as Spitfire and Hurricane pilots could. Undoubtedly this prison-like environment contributed to the high number of Emil landing accidents. However the Bf 109E did have a small clear-vision panel on the port side of the greenhouse which enabled Luftwaffe pilots to continue flying at high speed in bad weather, whilst Spitfire and Hurricane men had to reduce speed before they could roll back their canopies for a better view. The Emil's semi-reclined seating position feels odd, too, though Luftwaffe pilots apparently liked it, and it would certainly have helped give them an increased tolerance to *g* forces, a fact reflected by the adoption of reclining seating on modern jet fighters such as the F-16 Fighting Falcon.

On take-off the Emil's gawky, narrow-track gear demanded sensitive footwork and a gentle throttle hand to avoid a swing developing, but happily the powerful, light fighter had a very short take-off run. Climb-out, and indeed almost every flight regime, was tiring on the pilot's left leg though, because the Bf 109E had no rudder trim, and constant foot pressure was needed at high speed and high power settings to counteract the torque effect of the propeller. This was a curious and unnecessary omission, since contemporary British fighters did have adjustable rudder trim, and such a system is neither complex nor heavy. At high speed the Emil cannot have been pleasant to fly. Its ailerons became so heavy that roll manoeuvres required near-super-human strength, while the elevator stiffened to the point that a pull-out from a high speed dive could only be made very gently, which was perhaps as well because the aircraft had a record of structural failure in the wings and tail unit, the latter having external strut bracing which was outmoded even before it entered service.

In the whirling maelstrom of combat the Emil did have the advantage. It could turn more tightly than either Hurricane or Spitfire, with a turning radius of about 750 feet at 300 mph. An Emil pilot could pull a tight turn without much fear of stalling or spinning out, even at slow speeds, thanks to the British-invented Handley Page slats which popped out from the leading edges of the wings and served as useful stall warners, whilst also enabling the Bf 109E to climb slowly and steeply, making it difficult for pursuing British fliers to keep the aircraft sighted. But the slats had one disadvantage: as they popped in and out they caused the aircraft to yaw, and this weathercocking motion was not conducive to accurate gun-aiming.

Perhaps the Emil's greatest asset was the fuel-injection system of its Daimler-Benz engine, which enabled Luftwaffe pilots to escape a pursuer by pushing over into a dive. The normally-carburated Rolls-Royce Merlins powering Spitfires and Hurricanes would splutter and cut out momentarily in such a manoeuvre as negative *g* loads starved the engine of fuel. Consequently RAF pilots developed a technique of half-rolling into a dive,

thus keeping positive *g* forces on the fuel system, but giving an escaping (or pursuing) Messerschmitt a positive and often decisive edge. On the other hand the Emil's greatest disadvantage during the Battle of Britain was its limited range. At best it was good for about 20 minutes' combat after crossing the English Channel, less if — as was often the case — the fighters were unwisely employed as top cover for heavy, sluggish Messerschmitt Me 110s as well as for the bomber formations. Many Luftwaffe Emil pilots discovered this failing too late and were forced to ditch on their return trips to bases in Northern France.

On balance the Emil and early marks of Spitfire were evenly matched at mid-altitudes when flown by equally-experienced pilots. Above 20,000 feet the more manoeuvrable Messerschmitt had the upper hand. A British test pilot who flew both put it thus: 'The Bf 109E flew as though on rails; the Spitfire was as sensitive as a fiery horse.' Both were thoroughbreds.

The Bf109E's cockpit was cramped, especially for tall pilots, but the reclined seating position helped *Emil* pilots tolerate high *g* forces.

85

Supermarine Spitfire

Genius is rarely content within the fetters of convention, uneasy within the mind-narrowing bonds of rigid specification. Take Reginald Mitchell, a man who in the 1930s knew as much if not more than anyone about the arts of streamlining, of structural stressing, control surface flutter and the many other special problems associated with high-speed flight. Mitchell, quiet, unassuming, tweed-suited, pipe-smoking chief designer for the Supermarine Company, had designed the S.6B racing seaplane which had won the Schneider Trophy outright for Britain and set a world speed record of 407.5 mph in 1931, yet the bureaucrats asked him to design a four-gun fighter aeroplane with an open cockpit and fixed undercarriage. He did design it, but he was never happy with the Supermarine Type 224, whose specification was too tightly drawn, too dated for his wide-ranging mind.

Privately Mitchell reworked the design, retaining the 600 hp steam-cooled Rolls-Royce Goshawk engine, but incorporating a new wing, fully-enclosed cockpit and retractable landing gear. Then came news that Rolls-Royce would soon have available a new liquid-cooled 1,000 hp V-12 engine. And the Air Ministry had changed its mind again. The Royal Air Force's new fighter must have eight guns, and should be capable of flying at 275 mph at 33,000 feet.

Back to the drawing board went Mitchell and his design team, to fashion the smallest possible airframe around the new Rolls Merlin engine, whose slim ducted radiator enabled them to reduce the aeroplane's frontal area by 40 percent. The Supermarine Type 300, submitted to the Ministry in November 1934, had flowing lines virtually unbroken from nose to tail, and a thin wing of perfect elliptical planform. A prototype contract for one aircraft was awarded two months later and the first Type 300 made its maiden flight from Eastleigh near Southampton on 5 March 1936, flown by the Vickers group's chief test pilot, 'Mutt' Summers. Within weeks the Type 300 had been flown at 349.5 mph, and two months after the prototype's first flight a contract for 310 aircraft had been placed and a name chosen: *Spitfire*. 'Just the sort of bloody silly name they would choose,' huffed Mitchell, who was never to see a production Spitfire fly. Even as the prototype flew that spring morning he was dying of a stomach cancer which two operations had failed to contain. He carried on with production design work, but finally succumbed on 11 June 1937 after handing over to Supermarine's chief draughtsman, Joseph Smith.

The government order, increased to 510 aircraft in 1937, had Vickers-Supermarine's small factory on Southampton Water in a flap. Unlike the Hurricane, the Spitfire, with its stressed-skin monocoque airframe and complex curvature and subtlety of line, was ill-suited to mass production, and Supermarine was only a small business anyway. (It has been estimated that it took the equivalent of three average working lifetimes, about 330,000 man-hours to manufacture one Spitfire). Despite an expanded labour force, when Spitfire production got under way in March 1937 Supermarine built fuselages only, subcontracting all other components. Even then it soon became apparent that their combined efforts could not meet demand for the aeroplanes, so a 'shadow' factory was planned for Castle Bromwich near Birmingham, and a further contract for 1,000 Spitfires was placed before work had begun on the new plant.

The first Mark I Spitfires were similar to the prototype, but early service experience brought improvements: triple ejector exhausts instead of the flush stacks; a castoring tailwheel instead of a skid; and a 1,030 hp Rolls-Royce Merlin II

Standard Mark I Spitfire armament in the 'A wing' model consisted of eight 0.303 Colt-Browning Mk. II machine guns, each with 300 rounds of ammunition. The Mark IIA had improved Brownings whose fire rate was increased from 1,100 to 1,200 rounds per minute. 'B wing' Spitfires had two 20mm Hispano cannon in place of the inboard four machine guns but they proved troublesome in early trials through jamming feed and ejector mechanisms, and it was not until the Mark IIB appeared from Castle Bromwich in late 1940 that the cannon-armed Spitfire performed satisfactorily.

Mark II Spitfires had 1,175 hp Merlin XII engines, constant-speed propellers and 73 lbs of armour plate, but were otherwise similar to Mark Is. When Rolls-Royce made available the uprated 1,440 hp Merlin 45, many eight-gun Mark I and II Spitfires were brought up to Mark V standard, reputedly the best-handling Spitfires of all. Total production of Spitfires ran to more than 20,000, and Mitchell's inspired design fathered two dozen major marks. What was its special magic that it should still hold fascination for generations born to supersonic jets and space travel? It was the right aircraft at the right time, a distinctive shape with a defiant and evocative name which symbolized Britain's air power as the Messerschmitt did in Germany, the Flying Fortress in America and the Mitsubishi Zero in Japan. Yet, when war broke out in Europe Britain's air power was weak. Only nine RAF fighter squadrons had Spitfires, with two auxiliary units in the process of conversion training. A total of 2,160 Spitfires were on order, but less than half of the Air Ministry's hoped-for total of 300 deliveries had been achieved.

By July 1940, when the Battle of Britain started, RAF Fighter Command had 19 operational Spitfire squadrons and production was running at five per day — less than half the rate achieved for the less complex Hurricane. But it was the shortage of trained pilots which posed the greater problem. Prime Minister Winston Churchill's 'young chicks' were mostly desperately under-trained in the rush to get them operational, often with no more than a dozen hours solo on Spitfires after elementary training on Tiger Moths or Miles Magisters; and they were poor marksmen, easy pickings for the better-trained, well-prepared Luftwaffe pilots.

To such young men, in their late teens or early twenties, the Spitfire must have seemed very daunting after the light

Subtle curves and monocoque structure of the Spitfire are evident in this view. The rear view mirror on top of the windscreen was a vital piece of equipment in combat for spotting an attacker sneaking up from the rear.

engine driving a three-blade two-speed propeller instead of the fixed-pitch unit, upping the aeroplane's maximum speed by 5 mph to 367 mph at altitude. Early in 1939 a new domed cockpit canopy was installed to give tall pilots more headroom. In tests during high-speed dives it was found that pressure differentials made it impossible to slide the hoods back in an emergency at speeds over 250 mph; a small knock-out panel was incorporated which, when pushed out, equalized external and internal pressure, and external armour-glass windscreens were provided at the insistence of RAF Fighter Command's Commander-in-Chief Hugh 'Stuffy' Dowding, who pointed out reasonably that if Chicago gangsters could ride behind bullet-proof glass he saw no reason why his pilots should not.

Cockpit of a Spitfire Mark Vb; the hinged control column with spade grip and thumb-button for gun firing can clearly be seen.

aeroplanes in which they had received their flying instruction. Nearly ten times the power, a slippery, knife-sharp airframe and an unfamiliar retractable undercarriage. The small cockpit, set right back above the trailing edge of the Spit's elliptical wing, was less roomy than the Hurricane's and in it you sat lower down so there was little chance of seeing anything for twenty degrees either side of the nose when taxying unless you weaved from side to side and poked your head out of the open canopy. Prolonged taxying was prohibited anyway because the radiator temperature would rise sharply, and if the coolant boiled you would have to shut down and be pushed or towed back to dispersal, where the ground crew would collect a fine off you to discourage your carelessness. If you taxied with the flaps down, where propeller-blown debris could damage them, or with the cockpit door unlatched and banging against the fuselage skin, it was five shillings. Land with your undercarriage still tucked up, or use too much brake and tip your Spitfire onto its nose, and five pounds went to the repair crew. Like the Messerschmitt Bf 109E, a Spitfire needed careful handling on the ground. Some RAF stations kept crash crews perma-

nently waiting by runways with ladders and lengths of rope with which to recover Spitfires upended by heavy-handed pilots.

But in the air not a hint of clumsiness. Few aircraft have ever rivalled the Spitfire's handling. In the hands of a skilled pilot the light, near-perfectly harmonized controls and the 'oneness' of the machine made flight a joyful, lyrical thing. The cockpit environment felt 'right'. The control stick, hinged at the top for roll control, had a big spade grip with a brass gun-button falling conveniently under the left thumb and a trigger lever for the brakes. The rudder pedals were individually adjustable and the throttle lever had a good large grip, though the location of the undercarriage selector over on the right side meant swapping stick hands to retract the wheels after take-off and was a sure giveaway for an inexperienced pilot, whose Spitfire wobbled when he reached over to it.

The Spitfire 1A, which was the principal version used in the Battle of Britain was just a fraction faster than its Messerschmitt adversaries, on paper at least, and because of its greater wing area a Spitfire pilot who dared pull enough g should have been able to turn steeper and

Lyrical portrait of a cannon-armed Spitfire rolling. What red-blooded pilot could resist the temptation?

more tightly than an Emil pilot, but in practice the less-experienced RAF fliers, who were used to slow and unresponsive trainers, would back off under unfamiliar and uncomfortable high g loads, giving away that advantage. At high altitudes, above 20,000 feet, the German aircraft was a superior performer to the early marks of Spitfire. And it had the advantage of a fuel-injection engine, whilst the Merlins in Spitfires and Hurricanes had simple float carburettors which would cause them to cut out if negative g was imposed. A Messerschmitt was thus able to escape a pursuing Spitfire by pushing over into a steep dive. To follow, the Spitfire pilot would have to half-roll inverted and dive, keeping positive g on the aeroplane.

So, back in the summer of 1940, if you had survived your first fraught weeks on squadron, your day would start early, before sun-up, and long before sleep had washed away the accumulated weariness of 15-hour days on operations. Out of bed, sign the orderly's chit to acknowledge his early call, down a mug of tea then into your battle-dress: standard

RAF-blue uniform, a roll-neck sweater which chafed your neck into fighter-pilot's rash from the constant swivelling of your head while looking for bandits, and over to dispersal to collect your fleece-lined Irvin flying jacket, helmet, gloves and buxom Mae West lifejacket. Standing patrol today, so straight out to the aircraft. Your groundcrewman helps you on with your parachute pack and fastens the X-straps of your Sutton harness. He has already done a preflight inspection and run-up the Merlin at first light. He plugs in the trolley accumulator, gives you a thumbs-up, and you stroke up the primer and press the starter button. Six exhaust stubs belch out shotgun blasts of blue-grey smoke, the Merlin catches, and the crewman waves you away. You bounce briefly across the bumpy grass airfield in loose formation with two other Spits, hold low, accelerating while you flip the brake lever to halt the wheels' spin before selecting gear up and making angels (the RAF slang term for climbing fast) with the seat racked down and the canopy closed, taking a quick whiff of 100 percent oxygen to clear

left
Spitfire V of the Royal Air Force's Battle of Britain Memorial Flight.

below
The narrow-track undercarriage of the Spitfire is noteworthy in this sharp-end view. Four-bladed propeller instead of three blades and six instead of three exhaust stacks on each side are latter-day additions to this early Mark Ia.

your head, ready for the to-and-fro, caged-animal stalk of your patch of sky and looking forward to bacon and eggs for breakfast when you get back. Unless there was a 'flap' on. Then you might just have time to relieve your bursting bladder while the fuel bowsers filled your Spitfire's tanks and the armourers her ammunition bays before taking off again. Or it might be one of those long, tense days of lounging in the broiling sunshine, still full-kitted out for the cold at 20,000 feet, too keyed up to concentrate on the pages of *Picture Post* or *Lilliput*, and with an ear ever-cocked for the ring of the phone line from Operations or the stomach-lurching click of the tannoy loudspeaker before the *Scramble!* call comes and you run, dragging your 'chute through the grass, to your Spitfire, which the groundcrew has already started up. 'Soon be bedtime!' your fitter calls. Cheeky blighter, what's he got to be so cheerful about? But he's right. Noon now. Another eight or nine hours and the daylight will be gone. Maybe down to the village pub for a pint or two, then blessed sleep. Standing patrol again tomorrow.

Hawker Hurricane

People were trying to shoot down Sydney Camm's new fighter long before it had ever flown. In 1933 Camm, chief designer for the Hawker Aircraft Company and creator of the Hawker Fury biplane which was then the Royal Air Force's front-line interceptor, revealed to the Air Ministry his plans for a High Speed Fury Monoplane fighter. Members of the Air Council, who would have to approve the funding for such a project, were sceptical. At £5,000 each the new aeroplanes would be too expensive, they pointed out. Taxpayers would never stand for it. Besides, the fighter was too heavy. Its wing loading was too high. Pilots would not be able to handle it. No engine existed to power it. And moreover, they did not want it.

Unabashed, Camm proceeded with his design as a private venture, with full support from Hawker's board. Within a year the Ministry had changed its mind, as government departments are wont to do. Rolls-Royce had a new 1,000 hp PV-12 aero engine under development, and a 300 mph monoplane fighter was now an obvious possibility, even to the hidebound bureaucratic mind. Camm swiftly redesigned his proposed Fury Monoplane around the new powerplant and re-submitted the machine for ministerial approval.

The Air Ministry was set on an eight-gun fighter. Assuming that only rifle-calibre armament would be available, government scientists calculated that it would take a minimum of 250 hits to bring down an enemy bomber. Two seconds was about the longest period a pilot might be expected to keep a target within his sights, and 1,000 rounds per minute was the average fire rate for each gun; thus to get in 250 shots in two seconds, eight guns would be needed. The more guns, the better the chances of

Wartime Hurricane production at Hawker's Brooklands, Surrey, factory.

an average marksman (which most pilots were) scoring a kill.

Camm's presentation was for a four-gun fighter, but a contract for a single prototype was awarded, and this machine, to specification F.36/34, first flew on 6 November 1935 in the hands of Hawker's chief test pilot P. W. S. 'George' Bulman. 'It's a piece of cake, I could even teach you to fly her in half an hour,' he told Camm after the maiden flight.

Camm himself had doubts about the aircraft and later admitted that he feared it might be a failure. Given more time he believed he could have designed a thinner, more efficient wing, which might have made his fighter the greatest of all time.

Hawker's chairman, Thomas (now Sir Thomas) Sopwith, had no such reservations. So pleased was he with early trials reports that in March 1936 he ordered material stocks and bought-in components for an unprecedented 1,000-airframe production run, even before the RAF had conducted flight tests, much less placed an order for the aeroplane. It was a considerable gamble, but one which paid off three months later when the Air Ministry placed an order for 600 aircraft — fewer than Sopwith had hoped for, but still the largest order ever placed for a British aeroplane in peacetime.

Delays in delivery of 1,030 hp Rolls-Royce Merlin II engines set back RAF Fighter Command's plan to have 500 of the aircraft, named Hurricane at Camm's suggestion, in service by March 1939. The first production Hurricane, armed with eight 0.303 Browning machine guns, was delivered to 111 Squadron based at RAF Northolt near London on 17 December 1937. Within eight weeks all 16 of the squadron's aircraft were operational. On 10 February 1938 the commanding officer of 111 Squadron, Squadron-Leader John Gillan, flew from his base to RAF Turnhouse near Edinburgh on a routine familiarization flight. On the way to Scotland Gillan bucked a fierce head-wind, but the wind-assisted 327-mile return trip was accomplished in just 48 minutes. Gillan's average speed of 408.7 mph was widely acclaimed in the popular press. Much later it was revealed that official secrecy had obscured his true

Sir Sydney Camm.

Sydney Camm's High Speed Fury, arguably one of the world's most beautiful biplanes, from which the Hurricane design evolved.

average of 456 mph. Literally riding a Hurricane in both senses, Gillan's groundspeed had at times topped 500 mph, and he was thereafter known as 'Downwind' Gillan.

The Hurricane's service entry was not without incident. Pilots accustomed to slow, docile biplanes found the monoplane difficult to handle. In one year 80 Hurricanes were damaged or destroyed in accidents, mostly due to pilot error. A number of Hurricane pilots died in high speed crashes, apparently as a result of letting the streamlined, fast-accelerating fighter get away from them in dives, then pulling so much *g* in attempting to recover that they blacked out and lost control. The high *g* force which could be induced by injudicious use of the control column in the new fighters was something entirely new to squadron pilots. Few of the losses were attributed to the aircraft itself, though in early weeks of service Hurricanes mysteriously shed the filler caps from a small gravity-feed petrol tank located just ahead of the cockpit, dousing the unfortunate pilot in high octane aviation fuel and on several occasions setting the aeroplane alight when the streaming fuel was ignited by the hot exhaust gases. A spring-loaded filler cap solved the problem.

During the Munich crisis of September 1938 only three RAF squadrons were equipped with Hurricanes, a reflection of the dismal state of Britain's preparedness for an inevitable war. Had designers like Camm and Reginald Mitchell not forged ahead with projects despite official apathy, the situation would have been near-comic. The Munich agreement bought time: a year in which the Air Ministry ordered another 1,000 Hurricanes, Hawker's main factory at Brooklands geared up to produce eight aircraft per week, and licence production agreements were drawn up with the Gloster Aircraft Company and with the Canadian Car & Foundry Company in Canada.

When war was declared in September 1939 16 front-line RAF fighter squadrons had Hurricanes on strength, yet despite the urgent need to strengthen Britain's defences, Hawker had been encouraged to seek export markets for the Hurricane and had manufactured aircraft for Belgium, Persia, Poland, Romania, Turkey and Yugoslavia.

It is one of the unjust ironies of fate that while the name of Reginald Mitchell's Spitfire is synonymous with the Battle of Britain, Hurricane pilots actually shot down the greater number of enemy aircraft, accounting for more than the total destroyed by all other defences combined, including anti-aircraft fire. The 'Hurribox', slower than the Spitfire and with inferior high-altitude performance, was the bomber-killer, despatched to rout the Luftwaffe bombers while Spitfires tackled the fighter cover on high.

The Hurricane was a very different aeroplane to the Spitfire. It was bigger, sturdier, but some 40 mph slower than equivalent early marks of the Supermarine fighter, with a maximum speed of

A presentation Hurricane IIC 'British Prudence'. Note the 20mm cannon armament and underwing long-range fuel tanks.

opposite
The thick wing, humpbacked fuselage and 'greenhouse' canopy of the Hurricane are evident in this view of the Royal Air Force Battle of Britain Memorial Flight's Mark II, the last Hurricane built.

324 mph at 16,000 feet. Its maximum operating altitude was theoretically 30,000 feet, but anywhere above 20,000 feet the Hurricane's performance was hardly sparkling, prompting this squadron song to the tune of the negro spiritual *Ain't gonna grieve my Lord no more:*

You'll never go to Heaven in a Hurricane
  One,
You'll stall before your journey's done,
Oh, you'll never get to Heaven in a Hurri One,
You'll stall before your journey's done,
I ain't a'gonna grieve my Lord no more.

But Camm's design had qualities which compensated for lack of performance. The Hurricane had an old-fashioned structure. Its fuselage consisted of a welded steel tube frame with a secondary structure of wooden formers and stringers. The thick wing had two spars joined by a Warren-truss bracing and on the first Hurricanes was fabric covered, though Camm introduced stressed-skin metal-covered wing panels early in the production run. Although the Hurricane may have lacked the aesthetic appeal of Reginald Mitchell's masterly monocoque structure, it was easier, quicker and cheaper to build than the Spitfire, and equally important, its outmoded airframe was instantly familiar to any RAF fitter or rigger who had worked on Camm's Fury biplanes, so that damaged Hurricanes could frequently be repaired on site, while the more complex Spitfires had to be dismantled and returned to the factory or to one of Lord Beaverbrook's Civil Repair Organizations. So straightforward was the Hurricane's airframe that a CRO unit could often rebuild one completely in 48 hours. One of Beaverbrook's organizations is credited with replacing both wings and all eight guns on a combat-damaged Hurricane in less than two hours.

Hurricanes were popular with pilots. They were much less of a handful than Spitfires. The rugged wide-track under-carriage was more suited to rough grass airfields and bomb-damaged tarmac than the narrow spindly legs of the Spitfire, and the hump-backed fuselage profile and forward-set cockpit afforded better visibility on the ground. The Hurricane's cockpit was roomy and comfortable, though difficult to get into because the aeroplane stood so high off the ground and there was no strengthened walkway area on the wing root on which to plant your RAF-issue flying boots. Getting aboard demanded a practised technique using a dangling foot-stirrup, hand and foot-holds whose spring-loaded streamlining covers snapped at fingers and toes as you mounted the Hurricane's flanks, and often a 'leg-up' from your ground-crewman. Ground handling was less nervous than a Spitfire's, but a concentration of weight in the forward part of the aircraft combined with a light rear fuselage and tail structure and powerful brakes demanded great care to avoid nosing-over under sharp braking.

In combat the Hurricane's rugged airframe could absorb damage without calamitous failure and could be relied upon to get home, or at worst to hold together long enough for its pilot to make a semi-dignified exit. And for an injured or exhausted pilot the Hurricane was easy to set down on an airfield. At a constant rate of descent, airspeed around 90 mph and the Merlin throttled back and spitting and crackling like bacon in a pan, the Hurricane could be flown right onto the ground with but a single bounce before it would settle, solidly and reliably, on its wide undercarriage. Such an arrival in a Spitfire would at best be embarrassing

This view of one of the Royal Air Force Battle of Britain Memorial Flight's two airworthy Hurricanes shows the fabric-over-stringer rear fuselage construction and the ventral anti-spin strake beneath the tail section.

Exuberant demonstration of an export Hurricane I for Yugoslavia by Hawker test pilot Philip Lucas in 1939. Note the two-bladed wooden propeller of this early aircraft.

when the crash-crew arrived to drag the aeroplane away.

14,231 Hurricanes were built, but Sydney Camm's design never underwent the protracted period of development and improvement accorded the Spitfire, though it was subjected to bizarre modifications. Catapult-launched 'Hurricats' flew off specially adapted CAMships (Catapult Aircraft Merchant Ships) to provide fighter cover for merchant convoys in the Atlantic, and destroyed six Focke-Wulf FW-200 Condor maritime patrol bombers. It was a hazardous pursuit, because the Hurricats could not be landed back on the decks of the merchantmen; they had to be ditched alongside while a boat was launched to retrieve their pilots. During the Norwegian Campaign, plans were laid for ski- and float-equipped Hurricanes to operate off lakes. Most extraordinary of all was an experimental biplane Hurricane with a jettisonable upper wing panel which

provided extra wing area to lift heavy loads and could be ejected by explosive charges once the aircraft had climbed to altitude, reflecting the paradoxial principle that an aeroplane can fly with a heavier payload than it can lift from the ground. It was never used operationally.

The Hurricane has always played bridesmaid to the Spitfire's bride, but those who flew both appreciated their differing virtues. Wing-Commander Bob Stanford-Tuck, who commanded 257 Squadron with Hurricanes during the Battle of Britain, summed it up thus: 'My reaction to my first flight in the Hurricane after the Spitfire was not good. She seemed like a flying brick, a great lumbering stallion. But after the first few minutes I found the Hurricane's virtues. She was solid. She was steady as a rock and was a wonderful gun platform . . . Somehow she gave the pilot terrific confidence. You felt entirely safe in this plane.'

North American
P-51 Mustang

The very name spells America: Mustang, the fiery wild horse of the prairies. Yet paradoxically the best-known American fighter aircraft of World War II owed its origins to the British. In the spring of 1940 a British Purchasing Commission arrived in New York seeking new fighters for the Royal Air Force. The Curtiss company was unable to meet their demands for the P-40 Tomahawk, so the British delegation approached North American Aviation in California with a scheme to manufacture the Curtiss design under licence. No, said North American's president James H. 'Dutch' Kindelberger, but we will design you an entirely new fighter. Good, said the British. We'll be back in four months. Do have it ready.

They did. Kindelberger, his chief engineer John Atwood, and designers Ray Rice and Ed Schmeud designed and built the prototype NA-73X fighter in an incredible 117 days, though its maiden flight was delayed until 26 October 1940 by the late delivery of its Allison V-1710 liquid-cooled in-line engine. On its fifth flight the NA-73X flipped over on landing after the engine stopped because of fuel starvation. Test pilot Paul Balfour was unhurt, but the prototype was wrecked.

Fortunately, assembly lines were already being set up and a replacement aircraft was quickly readied, but it was only when the first RAF aircraft, to be known as Mustangs, were in production that the US Government took an interest in the aircraft and ordered two machines for evaluation by the US Army Air Force at Wright Field, Ohio.

In RAF service the Mustang was hampered by poor performance from the Allison engine's low-speed supercharger at altitudes above 20,000 feet. In the autumn of 1942 the US Air Attaché to

Invasion-striped P-51D Mustang is owned by a 'Colonel' in the Texas-based Confederate Air Force, pictured here during the CAF's annual airshow at Rebel Field.

98

London, Major Thomas Hitchcock, advised Washington that the Mustang's performance might be enhanced by mating a British Rolls-Royce Merlin engine with North American's cleanly-designed airframe. It was an auspicious partnership. The Merlin 65, with a compact two-stage integral supercharger, delivered 600 hp more than the Allison, giving an experimentally modified Mustang X a top speed of 433 mph. USAAF trials with pair of Packard-Merlin engined XP-51Bs were equally encouraging, and North American's plant at Inglewood began manufacturing P-51Bs for the US Army in August 1943. A second production line started up at Dallas, Texas two months later. Ironically, the Mustang's champion, Tommy Hitchcock, died in a Ninth Air Force P-51B when its wings broke off in a high speed dive over southern England in April 1944.

The first operational Mustangs delivered to the US Eight Air Force in England in December 1943 quickly established themselves as superlative escort fighters, accompanying B-17 and B-24 bomber formations on four and five hour missions, ranging 1,000 miles, then quite extraordinary distances for single-engined fighters. But the P-51Bs and Dallas-built P-51Cs had only four 0.50 calibre Browning machine guns. They lacked the immense firepower of the heavier Republic P-47 Thunderbolt, and in combat the framed 'coffin hood' canopy — and even the bulged 'Malcolm Hood' hastily retrofitted in the field — gave poor rear visibility. Two P-51Bs

were then taken off the production line in California and modified with stream-lined teardrop canopies. The aft fuselage area was cut down and the wing structure strengthened to take six 0.50s with a total of 1,880 rounds of ammunition and heavier external loads of bombs or fuel tanks. This bubble-topped P-51D had a more powerful 1,695 hp Packard-Merlin V-1650-7 engine. It replaced the earlier Mustangs at the Inglewood factory in February 1944, and at Dallas the following July, and became the best-known variant. 8,102 were built by North American.

The P-51D was more than half a ton heavier than the first Allison-powered Mustangs, and marginally slower in the climb and maximum speed than the P-51B (about half a minute longer to reach 30,000 feet and 5 mph slower, turning 437 mph) but its greater firepower made it more effective for ground-strafing of casual targets on the homeward run from escort missions, and it was superior to any contemporary German fighter in high-altitude combat. The loss of keel area from the cut-back rear fuselage noticeably reduced directional stability on early P-51Ds until a dorsal fin strake was installed to compensate. On internal fuel only the P-51D had a range of 950 miles, but underwing drop tanks carried on bomb racks could bring its total fuel capacity to 489 gallons, extending endurance to eight and a half hours and giving the Mustang a dry-tanks range of 2,080 miles. On short-range missions without drop tanks two 500 lb or 1,000 lb bombs, or clusters of three Bazooka-type

The Rolls-Royce emblem on *Miss Coronado* is a postwar affectation in tribute to the P-51D's RR Merlin engine. *Miss Coronado* is a restored Mustang owned by John T. Baugh in the United States. Like many currently flying P-51s it has been converted to a two-seater by removal of the radio equipment and armour plate which originally occupied the area behind the pilot's seat.

rocket launchers, could be carried, and the final 1,100 P-51D-25-NA aircraft off the California line (Inglewood-built Mustangs carried the -NA suffix, Dallas aircraft were suffixed -NT) had zero-length launchers for five-inch rocket projectiles.

The first P-51Ds reached USAAF units in England in May 1944, and they were most warmly received by pilots used to flying the heavier, cumbersome P-47. One squadron commander who protested that his men had no time to retrain on new aeroplanes was reassured by his own pilots: 'That's all right, general sir. We'll learn to fly them on the way to the target!' And they did.

The Mustang behaved just like its equine namesake. Sheer brute power as you poured on the coal for take-off, 61 inches of manifold pressure with the Merlin snorting like a bull, the huge four-bladed hydromatic propeller tearing at the air like a tornado as you barrelled down the runway pumping your feet on the rudder pedals to contain the torque, then soaring aloft at a breathless 3,475 feet per minute. This was some pony, but like all thoroughbreds it needed careful

above
P-51D cockpit. The empty space at the top of the panel would have been occupied by the gunsight. Small pilots needed cushions to see over the high cockpit coaming.

opposite
Cutaway view of a P-51D shows the six 0.50 calibre machine gun installation in the wings outboard of the fuel tanks and wheel-well area, and the Packard-Merlin's radiator assembly behind the wing beneath the fuselage national insignia.

handling and was quick to curb over-confidence. The lightest fingertip touch on the stick was enough, and woe betide the pilot who mishandled all that power, especially close to the ground. Rapid opening of the throttle, unleashing the Merlin's horses too suddenly, and the torque would snap roll the P-51 inverted in the time it took to cry *Oh Mother!* The Mustang demanded — and got — a pilot's attention at all times. No amount of trimming would persuade it to maintain straight-and-level flight on its own for long because is simply was not a stable aeroplane. Stable aeroplanes are hard to manoeuvre. The Mustang never was. It could out-manoeuvre any contemporary enemy or Allied type, except perhaps a Spitfire in skilled hands. The only factor limiting its ability to out-turn a pursuer was the pilot's tolerance of *g* loads. Late in 1944 Mustang pilots were issued with the first Berger 'Gee-suits', which squeezed the trunk and lower limbs under high *g* loads and prevented blood pooling in the legs, enabling P-51D fliers to make tighter

turns and steeper pull-ups without black-ing out, though as a result some Mustangs used to return from combat sorties with popped rivets and rather more wing dihedral than North American had given them.

Although the bubble canopy greatly improved pilot visibility, in clear sun-light at high altitudes, with sub-zero outside air temperatures, a Mustang pilot would nearly fry in the cramped cockpit. Swaddled in layers of thick clothing to protect him in the event of a high-altitude bale-out, he would swelter from the sun's rays and from the tremendous heat of the Merlin, separated from his cockpit by a dural firewall which contained neither its foundry blast nor its clamorous note. Pilots who had flown the earlier Allison-powered Mustangs found their engines smoother than the Packard-Merlin. Like all liquid-cooled powerplants, the Merlin was prone to battle damage. A single bullet or piece of shrapnel through its cooling system could put it out of action, and the P-51's under-fuselage automatic

P-51D Mustangs rolling down North American's Inglewood, California, production line. The 'D' Model was in production from January 1944 until August 1945 and was also manufactured in Dallas, Texas, and by Commonwealth Aircraft Corporation in Australia.

'Cottonmouth' is a privately-owned P-51D Mustang finished in spurious Royal Air Force markings. Note the huge paddle-bladed propeller and the radiator scoop beneath the aircraft's belly.

airscoop door was occasionally prone to malfunctions at inconvenient moments, resulting in a total coolant loss (and thus of power also) unless the pilot was quick to spot the rapidly rising temperature gauge in the (literal) heat of combat. If not, a bale-out was sure to follow, and that was difficult in the P-51D because a peculiarity of air circulation around the cockpit with the canopy open tended to trap his body behind the armour plate against the radio compartment. The only sure way to bid farewell to a Mustang was to open the canopy, undo your straps, then roll inverted and fall free, followed by your seat cushions. Why seat cushions? Because some desk-flier in the Army Air Corps determined that fighter pilots should stand no taller than five-foot eight inches, and that was too short to see out of the bubble-top canopy on the P-51D. Mustang pilots were thus categorized as one-, two- or three-cushion pilots according to their stature.

In the last year of World War II the Eighth Air Force in England had 42 squadrons of P-51Ds. On a typical escort mission, as many as 700 Mustangs would set off, carrying a pair of the 108-gallon compressed paper 'Baby' drop tanks which enabled them to accompany the bomber formations six miles high to targets deep in Nazi Germany. During the summer of 1944 the quality of Luftwaffe fighter opposition was poor; pilots were under-trained and lacked combat experience. Many Mustang pilots flew complete combat tours without a single air-to-air encounter. But when they did meet opposition the P-51Ds acquitted themselves exceedingly well. Lieutenant Charles 'Chuck' Yeager (the same Chuck Yeager as was later to become the first man to exceed the speed of sound in level flight, while testing the Bell X-1 rocket craft) destroyed five Messerschmitt Me 109s on 12 October 1944; Captain Bill Wisner shot down six

month later the Luftwaffe's first jet unit, led by 250-victory ace Major Walter Nowotny, lost four Me 262s to Mustangs, including its famous leader.

In thirteen months of European operations USAAF Mustangs destroyed 9,081 enemy aircraft (4,950 of them in aerial combat), nearly half of the total number destroyed by all American units in Europe between 1942 and 1945.

The P-51D also became the first American fighter to fly over Japan when aircraft from the 15th and 21st Fighter groups based on Iwo Jima escorted B-29 Superfortress bombers on a 1,500-mile round-trip mission to bomb the Naka-jima aircraft factory near Tokyo on 7 April 1945. One P-51D and one B-29 were lost in the raid against 21 Japanese fighters destroyed in the air.

After World War II, P-51Ds, which cost $50,985 new, were sold off surplus for as little as $3,500 apiece to air forces in South America, Africa, Europe, the Middle and Far East, and to private owners. During the Korean War some 245 Mustangs carried out ground attack missions against the Chinese in the first year of the conflict. One hundred and ninety four were lost to ground fire. Even in Vietnam some thought was given to employing a turbine-engined Mustang derivative as a counter-insurgency aircraft, and that project is not dead yet. Nor is the Mustang, still raced in the United States, and owned by former USAAF pilots, doctors, lawyers, accountants, businessmen, and others who appreciate the qualities of a thoroughbred.

Inglewood-built P-51D pictured during a factory test flight.

Focke-Wulf FW-190s on an escort mission on 21 November 1944, while Lieutenant Claude Crenshaw downed another five on the same mission; and Major George Preddy, the highest-scoring Mustang ace of the war, led his flight against 30 Messerschmitts en route to Berlin on 6 August 1944 and shot down six.

Although the P-51D was faster than the Luftwaffe's piston-engined fighters, it was no match for the rocket and jet fighters which attacked the bomber formations in the summer of 1944, yet, surprisingly, Mustang pilots scored victories over the 590 mph Messerschmitt Me 163 rocket fighter, and the 540 mph cannon-armed Me 262 twin-jet. On 16 August 1944 Lieutenant-Colonel John B. Murphy of the 359th Fighter Group destroyed an Me 163 over Leipzig, and on 7 October Lieutenant Urban Drew bounced two unidentified German aircraft over northern Germany and destroyed both before realizing that they were Me 262s. A

Lockheed P-38 Lightning

Lockheed's P-38 was a courageous venture for the company's first military fighter project. In one airframe, designers Hall Hibbard and Clarence 'Kelly' Johnson produced the first twin-engine single-seat interceptor; the first twin-boom fighter; the first with tricycle landing gear; the first to have turbo-supercharged engines; the first American fighter to exceed 400 mph in level flight; the first to make major use of stainless steel in its construction; and the first American fighter capable of being ferried across oceans to theatres of war under its own power.

But such a catalogue of innovation carried a high price tag, which was paid for by a lengthy and painful development period, an enduring (though largely undeserved) reputation as a hot and tricky 'problem ship', and ulcers for its creators.

The P-38 was designed to a US Army specification which called for a maximum speed of at least 360 mph at 20,000 feet, a one-hour endurance at combat altitude, and a take-off run of no more than 2,200 feet. Design work began in 1937 at Lockheed's 'Skunk Works' (so-named because of its black-and-white striped doormat) at Burbank, California. Kelly Johnson and chief designer Hibbard opted for a twin-engine configuration because there was no single powerplant available which looked capable of delivering the performance demanded by

This Lightning is a P-38H-5-LO. Note the exhaust-driven turbine wheels for the turbosuperchargers mounted atop the booms near the wing trailing edges and the radiators located either side of each boom.

the Army. They chose the radical twin-boom layout because it enabled the radiators and turbo-superchargers for the 12-cylinder Allison V-1710 engines to be located away from the main fuselage, providing a cleaner structure and a nose-mounted armament installation unhampered by the need for synchronization gear. The XP-38 prototype was to carry one 23mm Madsen cannon and four 0.50 calibre Colt MG-53 machine guns — heavy armament for its day.

On 27 January 1939 the prototype made its first flight after a secret, middle-of-the-night truck journey from the factory to March Field, California on New Year's Eve. Two weeks later Lieutenant Ben Kelsey zipped from coast to coast in seven hours, two minutes, including two fuel stops. The XP-38 touched 420 mph at times, but unfortunately came to grief in an emergency landing on a golf course near Mitchell Field, New York after both engines lost power on the last leg of the flight. By the time the first of 13 YP-38 production development aircraft had flown on 16 September 1940, large orders for the speedy aircraft had been received from the British Air Purchasing Commission and the US Army Air Corps.

The high-speed performance of the P-38 was a double-edged sword, however, bringing with it a problem which first manifested itself during wind-tunnel tests in 1938. Early in its service career the aircraft gained a reputation as a widow-maker when a number of P-38s and their pilots were lost in terminal-velocity dives during which the tail surfaces fluttered and eventually failed. Initially Lockheed's engineers thought the problem was peculiar to the twin-boom layout. In fact the P-38 was encountering a now

familiar problem to designers of high-speed aircraft, but then entirely new to Lockheed — compressibility. As the airspeed built up in a dive, at around 425-500 mph air would begin 'piling up' in front of the wing instead of flowing smoothly over it (trying to cut fresh bread with a blunt knife is a good analogy), shifting the centre of lift rearwards and causing the aircraft to tuck under into a steepening dive from which recovery was impossible. Lockheed test pilot Tony LeVier noted that compressibility was like 'a giant phantom hand that seized the plane and sometimes shook it out of the pilot's control'. Service pilots were little reassured by a Lockheed technical bulletin which claimed that the air was sufficiently dense for a pull-out to be effected at around 1,500 feet *below* sea level! 'I broke an ulcer over compressibility on the P-38', Kelly Johnson later admitted, 'because we flew into a speed range where no-one had ever been before, and we had difficulty in convincing people that it wasn't the funny-looking airplane itself but a fundamental physical problem.'

Johnson's solution was to change the incidence of the P-38s tail section and improve the fairing of the wing/fuselage junction. On the P-38J model, which was fastest of the series, small dive flaps were added to the outboard wing to further improve the aeroplane's dive characteristics. In March 1944 Ben Kelsey dived his P-38J to an indicated terminal velocity of 750 mph. Allowing for compressibility error in the airspeed indicator his true speed must have been close to 600 mph. The compressibility problem had been understood, and thereafter late model P-38s handled well at high airspeeds and

Fine frontal view of a P-38F emphasizing the clean airframe and unhindered weapons installation resulting from the twin-boom configuration.

were able to withstand high aerodynamic loads quite safely.

The P-38J, which first appeared in August 1943, incorporated the only radical external change to an aircraft whose production run spanned the entire period of American involvement in World War II. Combat experience on early model P-38s revealed the extreme vulnerability of their wing-mounted engine intercoolers to gunfire. Engine backfires could also cause serious wing distortion. So the P-38J featured core-type radiators beneath its engines. Gone were the aircraft's beautifully streamlined shark-nose nacelles in favour of chin cowls. Although the new radiators increased drag, enhanced cooling enabled the two Allison V-1710-89/91 engines to develop their full 1,425 horsepower at altitude, giving the P-38J a maximum level-flight speed of 420 mph at 26,000 feet.

Lockheed established a moving assembly line for the P-38J and later models, which greatly increased output of a complex airframe not ideally suited to high-volume production. No fewer than 22 sub-contractors were involved in manufacturing components for final assembly at Burbank, whence completed aircraft were towed through the streets late at night for flight testing at the Lockheed Air Terminal. So efficient was the system that by January 1945 432 P-38s were rolling off the line each month.

The availability of Allison's improved V-1710-111/113 engine with a war emergency power rating of 1,600 horsepower at 28,700 feet led to the P-38L, which was the major production model, 3,923 being built. The P-38L was armed with a single 20mm Hispano AN-M2C cannon, four 0.50 Browning machine guns, plus ten five-inch rockets or up to 4,000 pounds of underwing ordnance or stores — equal to the loads of early model B-17 Flying Fortresses. The aeroplane's extraordinary load-carrying ability inspired some unusual modifications, including one made by Hindustan Aircraft in India as a VIP transport for General Stratemeyer, which featured a glazed, leather-lined nose section complete with swivel seat and thermos flask. Cargo and personnel pods slung from bomb pylons were used by some self-sufficient groups in the Pacific for ferrying spares and ground crews, and on occasions hastily adapted drop tanks were used to evacuate stretcher cases beneath a P-38's wings.

To Luftwaffe pilots the P-38 was *Der gabelschwanz Teufel* — the Fork-Tailed Devil. To the French it was *Le Double*

Queue — the twin-tailed one. The Japanese had a charming symbol depicting two aeroplanes with but one pilot, while Americans and British knew it simply as Lightning, though some USAAF crews dubbed their P-38s 'Roundtrip Tickets' in recognition of the aeroplane's ability to get home after losing an engine. One P-38 returned to base five times on a single engine. Unfortunately, P-38 engine failures were not always (indeed, not often) caused by enemy action. The temperamental Allisons, whose turbo-superchargers gave the Lightning its characteristic 'whistle-while-you-work' whine, needed careful handling. Combat crews simply had no time to baby engines or pander to idiosyncracies in the heat of combat, and thus the much-vaunted twin-engine safety proved something of a myth. During one nine-month period of

service in England all Eighth Air Force Lightnings had at least one complete engine change. Another unhappy by-product of the twin configuration was the lack of engine-generated cockpit heat in the pilot's nacelle. Unlike his colleagues flying P-47s and P-51s, whose big engines were situated just a few feet ahead of the pilot's legs, guaranteeing a constant flow of warm air, the poor Lightning flier had to swaddle himself in a cumbersome 'bear suit' to avoid freezing at combat altitude. At least the P-38's counter rotating propellers assured an arrow-straight take-off run, with no torque factor to be counteracted with foot loads or rudder trim at high power settings, but pilots trained on single-engine aircraft were very wary of the loss of an engine on take-off or near to the ground. The P-38 was usually lifted off

around 95-100 mph, but the minimum single-engine control speed (the lowest speed at which the rudders had sufficient control authority to counteract the asymmetric thrust of a single engine) was 130 mph. The favoured technique was to lower the nose immediately after breaking ground in order to accelerate as quickly as possible, providing Lightning pilots with a valid excuse for indulging in a little low-level buzzing after take-off. To dispel the P-38's reputation as a killer with an engine out at low altitude, Lockheed test pilots Tony LeVier, Milo Burcham and Jimmy Mattern routinely demonstrated single-engine slow rolls into the dead engine at 50 feet — a technique not normally recommended for those who aspire to a long life.

In the maelstrom of combat the earlier pre-'K and 'L model P-38s suffered from a

This appropriately-marked *Der Gabelschwanz Teufel* is an immaculately-restored P-38L Lightning still airworthy with the Warbirds of America.

Twin booms of a P-38H make a natural frame in this delightful shot.

ponderous roll rate. Later variants had power-boosted ailerons which spared the pilot's arm muscles, and coupled with the aeroplane's Fowler flaps gave a greatly improved radius of turn. Skilfully flown, a P-38L could out-turn a Focke Wulf FW-190 or a Spitfire. Although the nose-mounted armament of the P-38 provided a narrower 'spread' of fire than the wing mounted guns of contemporary single-engine fighters, the concentration of fire was such that hits were almost sure to be lethal, and the superior visibility afforded by the twin engine configuration made sighting easier for the Lightning pilot. One feature of the aircraft which did not enamour itself to the first P-38 fliers was the tailplane, mounted between the booms immediately behind the cockpit nacelle, 'a cheese knife waiting to slice you in two when you bail out', one pilot opined. In truth the P-38 offered a better bail-out prospect than a P-47 or P-51, and there were very few instances of pilots beings struck by any part of the airframe when abandoning ship.

Although Eighth Air Force P-38s accompanied B-17 and B-24 bombers on long-range escort missions as far as Berlin, the aeroplane was only moder-ately successful in the European theatre of war, notably on low-level photo-reconnaissance missions with the Ninth Air Force. The Pacific was truly Lightning country, where the P-38's speed, range and high-altitude capability made it an ideal weapon with which to fight the Japanese over vast areas, operating with squadrons scattered from island to island. Nine or ten-hour missions were commonplace in support of bomber raids, and although the P-38 was less nimble than its principal adversary, the Mitsu-bishi Zero, the twin-engined fighter's superior firepower and speed, and the better training of USAAF pilots, enabled P-38 fliers to destroy more enemy aircraft in the Pacific war than pilots of any other Allied type.

Best known among top-scoring P-38 aces in the Pacific was the 49th Group's Major Richard Bong, who became America's highest-scoring fighter pilot of World War II with 40 kills to his credit (and probably as many more unconfirm-ed in the remoteness of the Pacific Ocean), all of them scored in Lightnings.

British Prime Minister Winston Churchill once remarked acidly that the P-38, which was not much liked by the

Royal Air Force, was 'a blessing quite effectively disguised'. Perhaps. Assuredly the twin-engine configuration did not provide the redundancy which it had seemed to promise, because a semi-crippled but still airworthy Lightning provided too tempting a target for enemy pilots. But the Lightning's ability to haul great loads over distances of two thousand miles or more was used to some advantage, and its heavy armament and concentration of firepower turned it into the most efficient ground-strafing aeroplane in the Allied inventory. That the P-38 was the only American fighter in production at the time of the Japanese attack on Pearl Harbour which was still being manufactured on VJ Day strongly suggests that Kelly Johnson and his skunk workers did something right.

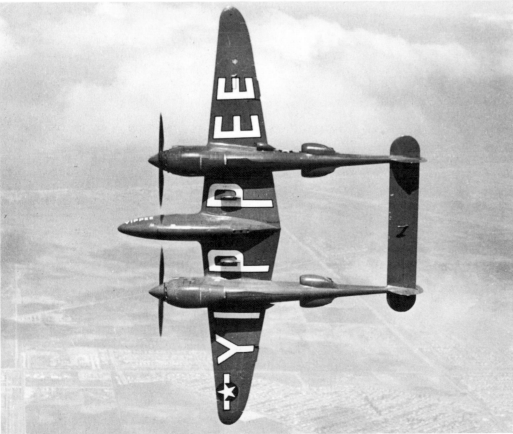

above
This restored Lightning is a P-38L. Note the 'chin' engine cowlings beneath the propeller spinners compared to the smooth 'shark nose' profile of the P-38H. Inner portions of the forward cowls were polished to enable pilots to make visual checks of the nosewheel leg position.

left
Yippee was the 5,000th production Lightning, a P-38J-20-LO built at Burbank, California. It was finished in firetruck red and widely demonstrated by factory test pilots Milo Burcham and Tony LeVier.

B-17
Flying Fortress

The earliest Flying Fortresses did not live up to the name coined by a Seattle newspaperman when he visited the Boeing factory. They were sadly under-armed, vulnerable to frontal attack, and had such a reputation for burning when hit that Reichsmarshall Herman Göring called them flaming coffins and 'Bomber' Harris remarked tartly that their armament was more appropriate to an amusement arcade than to a warplane. But not the B-17G, which was the best-defended Fortress of all, with 13 0.50 calibre Browning M-2 machine guns — two in each tail 'stinger', upper, ball and remotely-operated chin turret, and one at each waist hatch, nose cheek, and at the radioman's station, each with up to 700 rounds of armour-piercing ammunition.

In the 'Cheyenne' tail turret you squatted on your knees with legs doubled up for hour after numbing hour in the bomber's most important defensive position. That brought you little comfort because it was also the one which Luftwaffe fighter pilots invariably went for first. On earlier Fortresses the waist hatches had to be opened to fire the guns, in a 40-below blast against which you swaddled yourself in silk socks and inner gloves, woolly combinations, electrically-heated suit, flak jacket, fleece-lined flight suit and a tight-fitting rubber oxygen mask which itched miserably unless you shaved very close. If your Fort also had the older unstaggered waist positions you took great care not to tangle ammunition belts or oxygen leads with your back-to-back partner. At 30,000 feet a disconnected oxygen line brought death almost as surely as a 20mm cannon shell.

If you were the little guy on the ten-man crew you'd be a ball gunner, hunched embryolike in a plexiglas pustule below the aircraft's belly, from which you sighted your twin Brownings between your feet and fired them with arms arched

sharply above your head. At busy times the guns glowed red just in front of your face and the spent ammunition links piled like a junkyard on the floor faster than you could shovel them out of the chute. The ball turret was a key defence, but also a drag-ridden liability which knocked 25 mph off the Fortress's cruise speed. If you had to belly land the turret would break the bomber's back, so you spent a busy half-hour hammering and chiselling it free from its mounting so that it could

be booted overboard. In any case, though a B-17E or F might be bellied in with little damage, the G's remotely operated Bendix chin turret always dug in, pushing up and back into the fuselage, and there was nothing you could do about that.

Ahead of the ball turret sat the radio operator. Your prime function was to receive messages from base or Air Force divisional headquarters, and decode them from a rice-paper key-for-the-day which you would chew up if there was a chance of going down. You would help the navigator with radio fixes, transmit half-hourly position reports to enable your 'little friends' — the P-38, P-47 and P-51 escort fighters — to rendezvous with the formation, and fire the single flexible-mount 0.50 in the roof, though its poor sighting and narrow field of fire made it less than effective. You were also the crew's first-aid man, whose job it was to patch the wounded and comfort the dying. You'd fumble through the layers of high-altitude clothing to find a spot for the morphine needle or struggle to apply a torniquet in the bouncing, flak-rocked fuselage. It was also your unenviable task to balance like a highwire artist on the narrow catwalk across the bomb-bay to trip free any bombs which hung up on their racks, and to switch on the Fairchild K-24 strike camera which fired every ten seconds over the target, recording the destruction not only of the enemy but often of your own kind as well: haunting, obscene images of wrenched-apart Fortresses fluttering down like silver sycamore leaves, or disappearing in brief flashes of high explosive, gasoline, oxygen and human flesh — 30 tons of airplane and ten men gone in a shutter's blink, unwittingly and dispassionately captured in neat time-lapsed sequences.

The cockpit is dominated by the gate-like throttles for the B-17's four Wright Cyclone GR-1820-97 radial engines, which develop 1,200 hp each at take-off and are good for 1,380 hp at altitude thanks to their exhaust-driven General Electric B-22 turbo superchargers. Each

A low-level buzz-job like this would have been a grounding offence in World War II . . . if you were caught. This B-17G Flying Fortress *Sally B* is owned and operated by a group of enthusiasts in Britain as part of an Eighth Air Force Memorial Flight.

left
Cheek turret and remote Bendix 'chin' turret positions have been blanked off on this restored B-17G now operated by a group of Eighth Air Force enthusiasts in Britain. The bomb-aimer's position was in the forward glazed section of the nose.

Classic study of a Fortress formation with contrailing 'little friends' (escort fighters) weaving above on the look out for enemy fighters.

colourful splashes of individuality, the thinly-disguised *double entendres* to which the Army Air Force brass usually turned a blind eye: *Virgin-on-the-Verge, Heavenly Body, Mount'nRide, Grin-and-Bare-It* were perennial favourites, though some went for macho names like *E-Raticator, Knockout-Dropper* or *Murder Inc.*, and there was always an optimistic *Flak Dodger*. One Eighth Air Force pilot named all his Fortresses *Hang the Expense*. It was singularly apposite: he wrote off seven, at a quarter of a million dollars apiece. A good squadron artist could earn himself $15 a time for painting a copy of one of Alberto Vargas' perfectly-formed *Esquire* girls on the nose of a Fort. Occasionally, Air Force Command would try to censor the pin-ups, and you'd have your artist apply a tasteful swimsuit in washable paint for when the General came round. It always rained in England.

throttle is shaped like a capital F, and they are so arranged that the middle segments come together to form a common grip, which can be held easily in one thick-gloved hand and moved in unison or in any combination with finger-light finesse. You were glad of that at the start of a mission as you used differential throttle to steer along in the lumbering, swaying conga-line of Fortresses heading out to the runway. From behind, they looked like hump-backed eagles, row upon row, their olive drab camouflage relieved by

As you waited, the background throb of two hundred or more idling radial engines would be counterpointed by the rising and falling crescendo of Forts at take-off power. You took off at precise 30-second intervals, and with a gross weight often approaching 65,000 pounds you needed every last inch of the standard 4,400 foot USAAF runway before you began clawing up through the inevitable murk to make your 180-degree

right
Streaming contrails from the high-flying bombers gave away the massed formations of Fortresses to Luftwaffe fighter pilots. This view of a B-17G shows to advantage the chin and ball turrets and the aircraft's relatively small bomb bay.

112

left turn and follow the beckoning radio compass needle to the 'buncher' beacon, over which you joined up with hundreds of others in battle formation. Assembly altitude would vary with the weather, but was usually just below oxygen level. This was a dangerous time, for although you flew in precisely-ordered flights of six aircraft, comprising two vees of three, with each flight separated from the next vertically and horizontally, some goof always got lost and joined up late, or went the wrong way in the wheeling mêlée. Collisions were not uncommon, but with 12,000 pounds of high explosive and more than 5,000 gallons of high octane fuel aboard two Forts, they were over very quickly.

Each of the Fortress's engines fed off its own 354-gallon fuel tank. Long-range, so-called 'Tokyo' tanks in the outer wings provided an additional 225 gallons for each engine, but they were unpopular with crews when first introduced because leaks from the fuel cells caused gasoline fumes to build up in the wingtips and turned the entire wing into a live bomb if hit by enemy fire. Extra venting at the tips cured that problem.

Ahead of the pilot and co-pilot, right up in the Fort's plexiglas nose, sat the bombardier. It was your job to sight the target through the secret Norden 'Blue Ox' bomb sight. While training in the cold clear air over Arizona they told you that you should be able to hit a pickle barrel from 30,000 feet, but here over Hitler's *Festung Europa* the flak and fighters denied you that kind of accuracy. You had switches to open the bomb doors and release your Fort's load (6,000 pounds routinely, with a maximum overload of 12,800 pounds) singly or in salvoes. For all its size the Fortress's bomb load was miserably small. The weight of all that defensive armament and manpower severely restricted its payload and the space available for bombs. Your Royal Air Force 'chums' flying Lancasters could hoist up to 22,000 pounds of explosive. They composed a rude song about you over-paid, oversexed Yanks, and your beloved *'Big Ass Bird'*, to the tune of The Battle Hymn of the Republic, which went: *Fifty Flying Fortresses at Fifty Thousand Feet, Fifty Flying Fortresses at Fifty Thousand Feet, but they've only got one teeny, weeny bomb . . .*

The Fortress's 'office'. Note the big half-moon control wheels and the four 'F' shaped throttles which come together to form a common grip, easily adjusted with a thickly-gloved hand.

Four-a-burning, four-a-turning. Smoky start-up of the four Wright Cyclones of *Sally B*.

As you cruised at around 180 mph (the Fort was not a fast aircraft) at 25,000 feet, with condensation trails streaming from the turbocharger waste-gates to mark your passage for the Luftwaffe and your little friends, you tried to relax before the real work began near the target. On late model B-17s the bombardier could actually steer the Fort onto target himself, flying it via a link-up between the autopilot and his Norden sight. For the pilot a Fort was a friendly aeroplane, stable, forgiving and easy to hold in massive defensive pyramid formations thanks to those cleverly-designed throttle levers. Most B-17 pilots held constant power on the outer engines, keeping station with small adjustments to the inboards, The structure which Boeing designer Edward Wells created was a comfort too, for it would hold together after incredible punishment. The Forts were tough birds which would bring you home with fins and tailplanes gone, engines ripped out, fuselages nearly severed in mid-air collisions, or snapped control cables jury-rigged with parachute harnesses. Even

so, of the 12,731 Fortresses built by Boeing and peacetime rivals Douglas and Lockheed, who also manufactured the B-17, more than 4,000 were downed in combat, and to make up the terrible losses 16 B-17Gs per week were rolling from Boeing's Seattle plant alone during peak production periods. Losses reached their high point on 14 October 1943, when 60 B-17s were shot down and a further 101 damaged during a raid on the German ball-bearing works at Schweinfurt. Thereafter the swarms of Forts were escorted by long-range fighters when on deep-penetration missions, and were able to range as far as Czechoslovakia with fighter top cover all the way, drop-tanked Mustangs weaving left and right high above the ranks of bombers so as not to outpace them. It was the arrival of the long-range escort fighters, coupled with the incessant day-in, day-out bombing, which destroyed and demoralized the Luftwaffe, yet as one B-17 survivor puts it, 'If Hitler had not insisted on developing the Messerschmitt Me 262 jet fighter as a bomber we could hold our reunions in a phone booth'.

Huge fin and dorsal extension earned the Fort the nickname 'Big Ass Bird'.

A shiny new B-17E photographed on a test flight from the Boeing plant at Seattle, Washington.

North American AT-6 (Harvard)

At last! This was the day you had been waiting for, the day that would make it all worthwhile. The weeks of basic training, slogging round the drill square. The absurd class system in pre-flight school which forced you, a rookie cadet, to sit at attention at meal times and raise each forkful of food to your mouth in a ritual square pattern while keeping your eyes staring fixedly ahead. The sadistic officers who addressed you from a point one inch away from your nose while you tried hard not to look at their eyes and responded with one of the three replies permitted you: *Yes, Sir! No, Sir! No excuse, Sir!* Then your primary flight training, learning to cope with a Stearman biplane and living in fear of being washed out as a flier and sent to air gunner or bombardier school. And basic training, lurching through Texas turbulance in a low-wing Vultee BT-13 which soon taught you why its nickname was The Vibrator. Today you were going to get your hands on a *real* aeroplane for the first time, one that looked like the fighters on the recruiting posters.

The Navy fly boys down in Florida called theirs SNJs. The Limeys training up north in Canada knew it as the Harvard. To you and the Army it was the Noth American AT-6. If you were in the company of some lesser recruits you might even refer to it as 'The Six', implying a close relationship though you had never flown one. Only the aviation magazines and newspapers called it Texan.

And now the Army had decided to let you loose on one. It was waiting out on the flight line, polished aluminium skin shiny bright in the sunlight. Standing on its short undercarriage legs, with the big cowling over the 550 hp (five hundred and fifty horsepower!) Pratt & Whitney R-1340 Wasp radial engine thrust pugnaciously into the air, it had the stance of a bull terrier. The big greenhouse canopy seemed as high as a house, and the

Early Harvard Is for the Royal Air Force, distinguished by fabric-covered rear fuselages and rounded rudders and wingtips.

cockpit was a confusion of knobs and levers and switches which made your head spin. There was even provision for a machine gun on the starboard side, and the topmost limit on the airspeed indicator was 300 mph!

The AT-6 must have seemed a daunting brute to embryo fighter pilots, yet pilots training in Canada under British Commonwealth Air Training Plan went straight to Harvards after 65 hours elementary training on Tiger Moth or Fleet Finch biplanes, and eventually the Six was to lose its *AT: Advanced Trainer* designation and become a primary trainer, the first aeroplane which an American Air Force cadet ever flew.

The AT-6 was a development of a 1935 design by the General Aviation Corporation of Maryland. Designated GA-16, the open-cockpit, fabric-covered trainer prototype sired a line of US Army basic trainers culminating in the BT-14, a fixed-undercarriage closed-cockpit machine used by the US Army Air Corps, US Navy and the air forces of Britain, Canada and Australia, who were never happy with number-only designations and named it Yale. When the parent North American company devised a higher-performance, retractable-gear version, the BC-1 (Basic Combat trainer), the Royal Air Force and Royal Canadian Air Force took 230 between them. After Yale, what other name could they choose but Harvard?

The early BCs and Harvards had part-metal, part-fabric fuselage coverings, which gave way to all-metal skinning on subsequent variants. Late in 1940 the US

Army Air Corps adopted the AT-6 designation. They ordered 94 aircraft; the US Navy took 61 as SNJ-2s, and the RAF placed contracts for 600 Harvard IIs for the Empire Air Training Scheme. A modest start, but shortly demand for the AT-6 was so heavy that North American established a new plant in Dallas, Texas (hence the 'Texan' name) to supplement their California facilities, and Norduyn Aviation in Canada also began manufacturing the aircraft. The AT-6 was not classified as a warplane so no embargo was placed on exports. By 1942 it was North American's proud boast that pilots from 23 nations were training on their AT-6 throughout North and South

above
Running up a Royal Canadian Air Force Harvard IIA, finished in the all-yellow colour scheme which became familiar over Canadian skies during the massive British Commonwealth Air Training programme in World War II.

below
U.S. Army AT-6s on North American's California production line.

Six hundred horsepower was plenty to handle for a rookie pilot. This Harvard is finished in the colours of the Royal Canadian Air Force.

America, Europe and the Far East. And not just training. An armed Mexican AT-6B reportedly sunk a German submarine off the coast of Tampico, and the Royal Australian Air Force was using a home-grown armed version of the Harvard known as a Wirraway to fight Japanese Mitsubishi Zeros. Ironically the Wirraway bore a more than passing resemblance to the Zero and was frequently a victim of Allied fire (and much later, converted AT-6s were to star in the movie *Tora, Tora, Tora* as 'Hollywood Zeros'). Production continued throughout the war with the AT-6C (using plywood skin-ning for the fuselage to avoid depleting stocks of critical alloys) and the definitive AT-6D, which reverted to all-aluminium skinning

and was the major production model.

Four thousand three hundred and eighty-eight AT6Ds/SNJ-5s were built. In 1950 some 700 earlier models were re-manufactured as T-6Gs with improved canopies, additional fuel tankage and updated cockpit systems. Some were used in the Korean War as forward control aircraft, directing fighter-bomber strikes.

The AT-6 shares with the DC-3 a history of universal use. North American built 15,495 and supplied them to more than 40 countries. The aircraft was lic-ence-manufactured in Argentina, Aus-tralia, Brazil, Canada, Japan (by Zero manufacturers Mitsubishi) and Sweden. The total built worldwide is anybody's guess, for re-manufacture after the war has confused the records, but certainly was not less than 20,000, and for several decades the AT-6 and its sub-types was the standard military trainer. In some Latin American countries it still is.

You approached the AT-6 then with a lot of enthusiasm, a great deal of curiosity and a touch of fear. You had heard all the tales about what a nasty beast it was especially how it was ready to turn and bite the unsuspecting cadet in a vicious groundloop. Hadn't you even sniggered a time or two watching some other poor devil coming to rest in a dustcloud alongside the runway with a crumpled wingtip, a bent propeller and a badly bruised ego? Remember the cardinal rules, they said. *You're not through flying an AT-6 until you are back in the operations room,* and *There are only two kinds of AT-6 flier: those who have groundlooped one, and those who will.*

Groundlooping was the AT-6's only vice, and its cause was threefold. The short undercarriage legs were set close together on the flat centre section, combining a narrow track with a high centre of gravity. In a three point attitude the disturbed airflow from the wings tended to blanket the rudder, making it much less effective for directional control on the ground. And on the early models the tailwheel lock was released by full rudder pedal deflection. Thus, in the worst of all conditions, when a crosswind was blowing across the runway from the left (engine torque tended to make the aircraft turn left anyway), the AT-6 would try to weathercock into the wind, the student cadet would give a sharp jab of right rudder to correct, inadvertently releasing the tailwheel lock, and around she would go, scraping a wingtip, probably collapsing one undercarriage leg and turning the propeller into a passable imitation of a pretzel. At such times it was said that the two loudest sounds you would ever hear were the silence when the motion stopped and the wrath of your instructor from the back seat shortly thereafter. The preferred technique for painless landings was to 'wheel it on', keeping the tail up and the rudder effective for as long as possible, then applying gentle rudder and waiting for it to take effect without freeing the castoring tailwheel, which would ensure an uncontrolled pirouette. AT-6s were later modified to incorporate P-51 style tailwheel locks linked to the control column, which remained locked unless the stick was pushed full forward.

With all this very much in mind you would climb aboard for your first AT-6 sortie, noting the banks of unfamiliar switches along the cockpit sides, which the simple trainers you had been used to lacked. The Six felt right, one of those aeroplanes you strapped on rather than got into. Your instructor in the rear had virtually no forward visibility because of the steel tube roll-over frame between you which prevented the cockpit being crushed if the aeroplane flipped over on the ground. The AT-6 was designed to have fighter-like handling, and the Army brass, in their wisdom, thought that solo landings from the rear seat of one would give trainees a notion of what it was like to land one of the P-40s or P-51s to which they would graduate. But even the worst fighters had better visibility than the rear seat of an AT-6, and then there was the little matter of a 1,000 hp power difference . . .

Ready to start? You give her three shots of prime, call *Clear Prop!* over the side, then push your heel down on the starter pedal to get the inertia starter moving into its high-pitched whine before putting your toe down on the pedal

This beautifully restored machine is a North American SNJ-2, the US Navy version of the T-6/Harvard, finished in the colours of a training squadron based at Pensacola, Florida.

above
T-6 instrument panel, a
daunting sight for students
used to primary trainer
biplanes.

Many T-6C and T-6D aircraft
were remanufactured in the
early 1950s as T-6Gs, like this
one. Fewer canopy frames,
metal skinned control
surfaces, revised instrumen-
tation and radio equipment
and square-tipped propellers
(in an effort to reduce the
distinctive T-6 buzz-saw
howl) distinguished 'G'
models.

to engage the clutch, switches on, maintain fuel pressure with the wobble pump, and if you have set the throttle no more than one inch open she will fire up. Too much throttle and the Pratt & Whitney will snort and run raggedly, counterpointing each half-hearted burst of power with a great thunderous burping backfire like a flatulent popgun. Enough fuel? The gauges are beside your seat, set beneath glass windows which have become so obscured by all the dust and muck that settles in the cockpit that you can scarcely read them, and in any case the flight manual advises that their 'values should be regarded as approximate'. They are to be gazed upon with even greater suspicion from the rear seat, where parallax error will create an unwarranted sense of optimism about your fuel state. Luckily there is a red warning light on the panel which will flash whenever either of the two 55 gallon fuel tanks holds less than 10 gallons, enough for about 20 minutes flight. You taxy out in a line of other silver AT-6s, rudders waggling like a row of ducks' tails as their pilots weave left and right to see ahead. Last week an inattentive cadet sawed the tail off the aeroplane he was following.

Aloft in the practice area you discover the true nature of an AT-6. It is no straight-and-level aeroplane, why, she just *begs* to be aerobatted. The controls are light, fingertip jobs, just like a fighter's. She'll go over a loop beautifully from a shallow dive to 180 mph, describing a big smooth graceful circle in the sky, but be careful not to apply too much stick pressure. This is no sluggardly Bee Tee and you don't want to black out. Barrel roll? Oh, delightful. A great lazy sweep like a porpoise playing in the ocean. This is going to be a great aeroplane to fly.

And it was going to be your classroom, too, in which you would learn the secret arts of instrument flying, under a canvas and aluminium hood like a perambulator cover in the rear seat, while your instructor sat up front with a good view for a change. Then there would be gunnery training. The AT-6 could be kitted out with three .30 calibre Browning M-2 machine guns, one alongside the starboard cowling, one in the starboard wing root, and a third on a flexible Scarff ring in the rear cockpit, whose bucket seat could be swivelled round to provide a gunnery station (That facility, and a fold down rear canopy, makes a T-6 an aerial camera ship par excellence, and surviving examples are much used for air-to-air photography and filming). Your target would be a banner (or sleeve if you were a Navy man)

towed by another AT-6. Your gunnery instructor had drilled you most thoroughly: *Don't shoot the banner off the tow-plane; don't shoot down the tow-plane* (it happened); *don't get fixated on your target and fly into it, or into the ground* (as this was likely to spoil your whole day); *and try not to shoot off your own propeller.* The cowl-mounted Browning was synchronized to fire between the revolving propeller blades, but the synchronization gear was prone to fail. Groundcrew became quite expert at reaming out .30 calibre holes in AT-6 propeller blades. The holes added a distinctive whistling note to the AT-6's standard buzz-saw drone, which would rise to a crescendo, a howling, wailing *yeeeeerooooowwww* at high rpm when the propeller tips went supersonic. Restored T-6s are not very popular with the environmentalists.

Yet these aircraft are held in great esteem by those who trained on them: 50,000 US Army Air Corps men, 40,000 US Navy fliers, and 49,000 Commonwealth pilots from Britain, Canada, Australia and New Zealand in World War II alone, and as many more in peacetime, during an extraordinarily long career of scaring, teaching and most of all delighting neophyte airmen the world over.

OK, son, now show me where your fuel pressure gauge is. A blindfolded cadet pilot gets checked out on his knowledge of the T-6's cockpit layout.

MiG-15

You will not find it on a map or in an atlas, but any United Nations pilot who flew in the Korean air war can tell you where MiG Alley was: a stretch of airspace above the Yalu River which separated Korea from Manchuria. It was in this area on 1 November 1950 that a flight of United States Air Force F-51 Mustang fighters and a T-6 target spotter were attacked by six unfamiliar swept-wing jet fighters which dived on them from across the Yalu, beyond whose banks the UN pilots were forbidden to stray. It was the first appearance in the six-month-old war of a weapon which was to come as a rude surprise to the British Commonwealth and American forces and whose name was to symbolize Soviet airpower for decades — the MiG-15.

Both the Russians and Americans had made good use of material gathered from German scientists after World War II. In particular the Germans had done some solid research into the problems of transonic (faster than sound) flight, and had concluded that the onset of the drag and control problems brought on by compressibility at high airspeeds could be delayed by sweeping the aircraft's wings backwards. In Russia the Mikoyan-Gurevich design bureau (hence MiG, after co-designers Artem Mikoyan and Mikhail Gurevich) drew heavily on work performed by Kurt Tank of the Focke-Wulf company, who at the time of the MiG's Korean debut was developing a look-alike jet fighter in Argentina called Pulqui II, also based on his original Focke-Wulf Ta-183 design. But it was the British rather than the Germans who helped get the MiG-15 into the air. In early 1947 Britain supplied Russia with a batch of new Rolls-Royce Nene turbojet engines, then not in service with any British aircraft, solving the MiG design bureau's major problem — a suitable

powerplant for the new interceptor. The first MiG-15 flew on 30 December 1947, three months later than the prototype of the American F-86 Sabre which was to become its principal adversary and ultimately its conqueror. Within a year of receiving the British Nene engines Russia had put a copy of the powerplant into production without troubling with permissions or licences as the RD-45F, which had a thrust rating of 5,005 lbs. A more powerful derivative of this power-plant, the 5,953/6,990 lb VK-1/VK-1A, was used in later MiG-15bis fighters and MiG-15 UTI two-seat trainers.

The MiG was a superior fighter to the F-51 Mustangs, F-80 Shooting Stars and F-84 Thunderjets used by the American forces in the early months of the Korean conflict, although on 8 November 1950 when F-80s and MiGs took part in the first ever jet-vs-jet aerial battle, it was an American, Lieutenant Russ Brown of the USAF's 51st Fighter Interceptor Wing, who drew first blood, while flying top cover for a formation of B-29 Superfortresses bombing North Korean positions on the south side of the Yalu. His kill was the first of 827 MiGs destroyed in the war (combat claims are notoriously unreliable, but this is the most often quoted figure). Nevertheless, Lt. Brown had been lucky; the new Russian fighter was clearly superior in speed and rate of climb to the straight-wing American jets.

above
Now far from MiG Alley, the MiG-15 in which Lieutenant Kum Suk No of the North Korean Air Force defected in October 1953 is now displayed in NKAF colours at the United States Air Force Museum, Wright-Patterson Air Force Base, Dayton, Ohio.

left
MiG-15s were armed with slow-firing 37mm and 23mm (one or two depending on variant) cannons mounted in a quickly-removable tray behind the nosewheel bay. Note the distinctive vertical flow-splitter in the aircraft's nose intake.

Soviet Air Force MiG-15s on parade.

The MiG was a stubby, bluff-looking fighter with a tubby fuselage whose gaping nose intake was characterized by a vertical flow-splitter ducting air down both sides of the fuselage to the RD-45 turbojet. Unlike Tank's Ta-183 design, the MiG had a cruciform rather than a high-set 'T-tail'. Armament consisted of one 37mm cannon and one (later two) 23mm cannon mounted in a quickly-detatchable weapons tray beneath the nose with the gun barrels straddling the nosewheel bay. There was little headroom in the cockpit for tall pilots (luckily most of the North Koreans and Chinese who flew in Korea were small in stature and wore only leather flying helmets rather than the 'bonedomes' American Sabre pilots had), nor was there any provision for adjusting the seating position other than by using cushions.

Subsequent examination of MiG-15s has shown that the aircraft was quite crude in many respects, with many of the giant 'Clydeside' rivets which characterize Russian aircraft, hand-operated pneumatic brakes, and power-boosting only on the aileron controls.

Nonetheless, the early encounters with this hitherto unsuspected interceptor left American pilots in no doubt that in experienced hands it could be a most formidable opponent, and all effort was made to speed F-86 Sabres into service in Korea. Four days after their

arrival, on 17 December 1950, the Fourth Fighter Group's F-86A Sabres scored their first MiG kill when Lieutenant Colonel Bruce Hinton, of the 336th Fighter Interceptor Squadron, poured 1,500 rounds of .50 calibre ammunition into a Chinese MiG and it went down. 'I got a good close view of his MiG,' he wrote in his combat report. 'It was a beautiful sportscar of a fighter. The silver aluminium of pure metal was clean and gleaming, no dirt on the underside from mud thrown back from its wheels. It looked a first class airplane.'

The MiG was a good aeroplane which commanded respect among the American fliers, though few of the pilots who flew them did. The North Koreans and Chinese were mostly under trained, lacking combat experience (many of the USAF fliers were combat veterans from World War II), and were woefully short of that most essential of fighter pilot attributes — aggressiveness. It was not uncommon for North Korean Air Force or Chinese MiG pilots to bail out when caught by Sabre pilots, even before they had fired a shot. The Russians were a different matter. Ostensibly 'volunteers' (in fact whole Soviet regiments were attached to the Chinese units operating out of Manchuria), many of the Russian fliers had served in World War II, including the legendary ace Ivan Kozhedub, who is said to have commanded a Manchuria-based MiG unit. These pilots were disciplined, determined, efficient and not shy about pressing home their attacks far south of the Yalu River. 'Identifying the nationality of these MiG pilots was a constant problem,' wrote Canadian pilot Bruce Hutton. 'To most fighter pilots the adversary is usually just an aircraft with evil insignia, with no thought given to its human contents. However, in the face of numerical odds, an aircraft with a greater rate of climb and ceiling, it's vital to know if you're dealing with an individual who has never so much as ridden a bicycle, or one who may have destroyed 100 Messerschmitts on the Russian Front a few years earlier.'

Numerical superiority was very much the name of the game in Korea. The

No Kum Suk's now famous MiG-15, the first to fall into American hands.

The same machine in full United States Air Force markings during extensive flight testing at Wright-Patterson Air Force Base in Ohio.

Communists had perhaps 1,000 MiGs at their disposal at any one time, and would put up formations of anything from 100 to 300 aircraft from bases just over the Manchurian border, to oppose F-86 formations which rarely numbered more than 60 or 70 aircraft. The Communists also had the advantage of operating very close to their bases, whereas the Americans came from bases south of the 38th Parallel. Even using external drop tanks the Sabres were frequently limited to a combat duration measured in minutes before someone called 'Bingo' (low fuel) and they would have to break off and go home.

How did the two aeroplanes measure up? On balance their advantages and disadvantages cancelled one another out, setting aside the question of pilot competence. The MiG-15 was intended primarily as a bomber interceptor. Its slow-firing cannons were excellent for attacking bomber formations but inadequate for air-to-air combat against other jet fighters. American pilots claimed you could actually see the shells in the air! It lacked the armour protection which F-86 Sabres had, and did not have the radar-ranging gunsights fitted to the F-86F. It was slower than either the F-86E or 'F (668 mph at sea level compared to 679 mph and 695 mph respectively) and despite popular belief to the contrary was incapable of supersonic flight, even in a dive. On the other hand, with much the same thrust available the MiG was some 7,000-8,000 lbs lighter than contemporary F-86s and could outclimb them (a MiG-15 had a maximum rate of climb of 10,100 feet per minute and a ceiling of 55,000 feet; the best of the Sabres, the F-86F, climbed at 9,300 feet per minute and had a ceiling of 48,000 feet). This edge in climb rate and ceiling dictated Communist tactics in Korea. It was usual for huge formations of MiGs to patrol over the Yalu River area at maximum altitude, where the Sabres could not reach them, then break off into small groups and come diving down through the American aircraft, making high speed

control. The F-86F had no such tendency, and though its six .50 calibre machine guns lacked the hitting power of the MiGs Nudelmann-Rikter cannons, its stability, superior fire-rate (1,100 rounds per minute compared to 450 and 650 rounds per minute for the cannons), radar-ranging gunsight, and better trained pilots made Sabre-vs-MiG a more one-sided contest than performance figures would suggest. Throughout the Korean War F-86 pilots destroyed 792 MiG-15s for the loss of 78 of their own kind, giving a kill ratio of 10:1. Figures released after the war and still quoted gave kill ratios as high as 14:1; others suggest that additional Sabre losses not then attributed to MiGs actually bring the figure to 8:1. It matters little; the figures are decisive.

Why then is the MiG such a remarkable aircraft? Why did it create the impression of power and superiority in Korea when losses were so high? Don't let statistics fool you. In the hands of skilled Russian pilots (the *Honchos,* as American fighter jockeys called them) MiG-15s were to be reckoned with. Their legend lived beyond the end of the Korean War — indeed so anxious were the Americans to get their hands on a flyable MiG-15 even after the war ended that they launched Operation Moolah, offering a $100,000 inducement to any Communist pilot who defected with his aeroplane. In October 1953 Lieutenant Kum Suk No of the North Korean Air Force landed a MiG-15 at the American Air Force base at K-14 Kimpo, collected an American Express cheque and told his welcoming new friends: 'But for the sheer superiority of your Sabre, I am sure the Korean War would still be going on today.' The MiG was evaluated in the United States in mock dogfights, yet the results of those trials have never been disclosed, perpetuating the myth which still brings the name MiG to mind whenever Soviet air-power is mentioned. Kim Suk No's MiG is now displayed at the USAF Museum at Wright-Patterson Air Force Base, Dayton Ohio.

The Korean conflict was just the beginning of the MiG-15's career. The aircraft was manufactured in Russia, Poland, Czechoslovakia and China in great numbers, probably in excess of 15,000 aircraft in fighter and trainer variants, known in that curious NATO codespeak adopted for Russian aircraft as *Fagot* and *Mongol* respectively. Many MiG-15UTI trainers remain in service with the air arms of third-world countries. Doubtless some still ply the cold clear air of MiG Alley.

firing passes before zooming back up to the safety of altitude, a technique known to USAF pilots as *yo-yo-ing* which had been used to great effect by Luftwaffe fighter pilots attacking British and American bomber formations. The MiGs, operating under radar direction from nearby Manchurian airbases, were also able to make quick dashes back to the sanctuary of the north side of the Yalu when they ran into serious trouble.

And they often did. The Sabre, especially the F-86F which had an extended '6-3' wing (so-named because the leading edge slat was replaced on this model by a smooth leading edge extended *six* inches at the wingroot and *three* inches at the tip) was a better flying aeroplane. Earlier Sabres had been unable to match the MiG in a high-altitude turn. The 'F could, and it was a far better gun platform. At high angles of attack the MiG's high-set tailplane would be affected by turbulent air from its wings, leading to a sudden loss of stability and causing it to pitch up violently, and sometimes to spin out of

Beech Bonanza

Bonanza is the Spanish word for prosperity or success. It was Walter Beech's choice of name for his first postwar lightplane, and though he never lived to see it (Beech died in 1951 leaving his widow Olive Ann to run the company, which she does to this day), the Bonanza was to become a symbol of prosperity in the field of personal transportation and set a record for continuous production.

In 1944 the Beech factory was heavily engaged building Staggerwings and twin-engine transports and trainers for military use, but like other manufacturers Beech was already planning for peacetime, when it was expected that many thousands of pilots trained for war would want to continue flying in private aircraft. Other companies were planning mass-production two-seaters with $2,000 price tags. Beech wanted something better. He knew that the outdated, labour-intensive Staggerwing would not survive long in the postwar market (20 G-17S Staggerwings were built after the war, but they were custom-made and cost $29,000 each). Nevertheless he believed his new aeroplane should offer the same qualities: speed, payload, range and comfort, at a price between $6,000 and $7,000.

When Beech put Ralph Harmon in charge of design studies, Harmon quickly scrapped a proposal for an undistinguished tailwheel aircraft, the Model 33. By November 1944 Harmon had sketched out his own ideas for the new Beechcraft, now designated Model 35. It was to be a four-seater with retractable tricycle undercarriage and a revolutionary V-tail with no vertical fin, just two tailplanes canted at an angle to one another like the partially-closed wings of a butterfly. Harmon had spotted a drawing of the butterfly tail in an engineering journal. The original idea came from a Polish designer. Far from being a mere gimmick

it seemed to offer a number of advantages: having two tail surfaces instead of three cut airframe weight, made manufacturing easier and reduced drag, while leaving control effectiveness unaltered. Beech conducted wind-tunnel and flight trials with a V-tail modifed AT-10 twin to confirm the theory. Walter Beech was not an engineer, but he knew a strong selling-point when he saw one. 'That's what we ought to build,' he told Harmon when he first saw his sketches, and as so often, Beech was right. The butterfly tail has been a unique distinguishing feature of the Bonanza among a confusing mass of look-alike aeroplanes for 35 years.

Beech embarked on the most sophisticated programme of wind-tunnel and structural testing that had ever been employed for a lightplane in developing the final design for the Model 35. A laminar-flow airfoil section was tested alongside the NACA 23000 airfoil used successfully on the Staggerwing and Model 18 twin (the latter won), and engine manufacturers Lycoming and Continental were asked to submit proposals for horizontally-opposed engines for the aircraft. An automobile stylist was hired to attend to detail design. The first Model 35 took off from Beech Field, Wichita, on its maiden flight on 22 December 1945, with test pilot Vern Carstens at it controls. 'It's the best airplane we've built yet,' he told Beech after the flight.

Bonanza trio: in the foreground is a current-model vee-tail Bonanza V35B, accompanied by two 'straight-tail' Bonanzas, the six-seat A36 *(left)* and F33A *(right)*.

The prototype Bonanza had a laminar-flow wing and a 165 hp four-cylinder Lycoming engine. Production aircraft reverted to the NACA airfoil section and were powered by six-cylinder 185 hp Continental powerlants. For 15 months Beech subjected Bonanza test airframes to every kind of indignity. Aircraft were flown continuously around a 170-mile circuit by a team of pilots who made an average of three take-offs and landings every hour for more than 500 hours. Wings were hammered non-stop by machines simulating the fatiguing processes of take-off, flight and landing, while Beech test pilots pushed the Bonanza to its structural limits in flight trials (and beyond — one machine broke up during high-speed dive tests, killing the pilot). Even before the first performance specifications were released Beech had received 500 cash deposits for the new aeroplane. When details were released and the aircraft had been certificated by airworthiness authorities as ready for customer delivery, Beech had a backlog of 1,500 orders. Some eager buyers placed six or seven separate orders with different dealers, while it was not uncommon for dealers to promise the same aircraft to a dozen customers. Production of the Bonanza was soon running at 12 aircraft per day even to keep one step behind demand.

Bonanza production in full swing at Beech's Wichita factory in 1947. In the background are Beech Model 18 twin-engined transports.

This Beech V-35B Bonanza is the current model, still in production after a record run spanning 35 years and more than 10,000 aircraft.

Why the eagerness to buy a new and untried aeroplane? Because the Bonanza *was* new, radically so. It looked exciting, challenging, with a charisma rarely matched by any other private aeroplane save perhaps the Learjet. It has a clean airframe, much of it flush-rivetted, with a roomy cabin protected by a strong rollover structure, and performance unrivalled by any other aeroplane in its price range (the 1947 model sold for $7,975). One mile per hour of cruise speed for every horse power is a rule of thumb much sought by light aircraft designers

and rarely achieved even today. The first Bonanza cruised at 175 mph on 165 hp. What is more, it could carry a full load over its range of 750 miles. Perhaps I should explain that unlike motor cars, light aeroplanes cannot necessarily carry all they have room for. Often if you want to fill the fuel tanks for maximum range you cannot fill all the available seats with bodies without exceeding the aircraft's maximum weight limits; a compromise is necessary. The Bonanza flew almost as fast, almost as far as the Staggerwing it replaced, on little more than one-third of

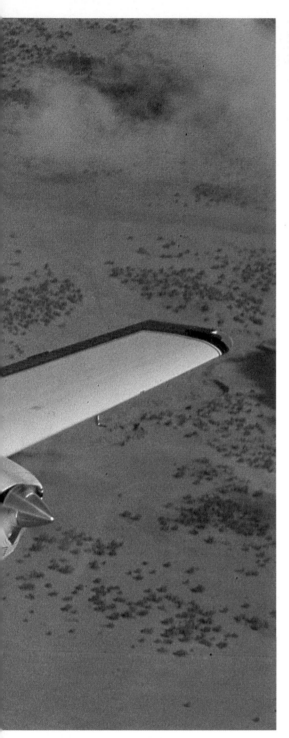

the worlds of haute couture and high finance. A bulk order was placed by Indian maharajahs, who saw the speedy Beechcraft as their best chance of escape in the event of peasant uprisings. Indeed the Bonanza had little competition. Its nearest rival was the North American Navion, which owed some of its design to the P-51 fighter but was no Mustang performance-wise. The Navion was 25 mph slower than the Bonanza, and North American had to sell it for less than it cost to produce, giving rise to the tale of North American president 'Dutch' Kindelberger telling a friend who asked if he could have a Navion at cost: 'Sure, we'd be glad to get the extra dough.' Apocryphal story has it that Kindelberger rode in a Bonanza just once, then told his colleagues: 'Gentlemen, we are out of the lightplane business.'

Bonanza sales were given a further boost in 1949 when Bill Odom set two world records in his *Waikiki Beech*, flying from Honolulu to Oakland, California, non-stop, 2,406 miles in 22 hours six minutes, and from Honolulu to Teterboro, New Jersey, non-stop, 4,957 miles in 36 hours two minutes. Odom was killed later that year when his specially-modified P-51 Mustang plunged into a house at the start of the 1949 Thompson Trophy air race at Cleveland, Ohio. *Waikiki Beech* made a record-breaking around-the-world flight in 1950 flown by a US Congressman, and is now preserved at the National Air & Space Museum in Washington, D.C.

During its unbroken 35-year, 10,000-plus production run the Bonanza has been subjected to continual improvement so that the current model V35B Bonanza bears only superficial resemblance to the first Model 35. Power has increased from 165 hp through 185, 196, 205, 225, 240, 250 and 260 hp to 285 hp, though only 28 mph has been added to the aeroplane's cruise speed. Structural and equipment changes have been numerous, and Beech's policy of making many of the latest Bonanza improvements available to owners of older models has been a boon to customizers. There are some 1947 Bonanzas flying which are externally indistinguishable from their 1981 brethren. Pride of ownership is very much a Bonanza trait. Rarely has any aeroplane attracted such fierce brand-loyalty. One man has owned 25 in succession. There is even an American Bonanza Society for fans of the Butterfly Beechcraft.

Not all Bonanzas have the V-tail. In

the horsepower. Beech's publicity of the day reflected the company's determination to sell to the upper end of the market. Bonanzas were pictured alongside the swimming pools of palm-fringed mansions, cruising beside Manhattan skyscrapers with sober-suited businessmen holding earnest conversations in the cabin, and depositing elegant ladies at the doors of limousines. 'The ladies', Beech noted, 'will much appreciate the retractable step which allows them to board while preserving their feminine dignity'. Bonanzas appealed not only to 1959 Beech introduced an economy model

A 1947 Model 35 Bonanza in standard plain-metal finish. The large rear cabin windows opened outwards for ground ventilation.

33 called Debonair which has conventional fin/tailplane surfaces. This model remains in production, though it now has the Bonanza name, and has sired a six-seat version called the A36 Bonanza which now outsells the classic V-tail by a handsome margin. Some measure of the sophistication of modern lightplanes (and the toll of inflation) may be gained from the knowledge that a lavishly-equipped A36, kitted out with every conceivable piece of avionics which could be crammed into its instrument panel, recently sold for $250,000. A $7,975 1947 Model 35 came complete with a single low-frequency radio. The clock was an optional extra.

In addition to the 20-odd production models which have sprung from Ralph Harmon's original design there have been a number of bizarre experimental models. In 1948 Beech test flew a twin-engined Bonanza, the Model 40, which had two 180 hp Franklin engines geared to a single propeller. This was an early attempt to produce a centreline thrust twin in which the failure of one engine would not cause control problems through asymmetric thrust, but it was not put into production. The Model 50 Twin Bonanza which appeared later was a true twin and had little in common with its namesake, though a San Francisco company did offer custom twin-engine conversions of the V-tail Bonanza as the Oakland Super V in the 1950s. During the 1948 Arab-Israeli War the Israelis used a Model 35 Bonanza to bomb Arab positions. A machine gun was mounted at one of the opening side cabin windows, and bombs were rolled out of the door! Armed versions of the straight-tail Model 33 Bonanza were tested by the United States Air Force during the Vietnam War and Model 36s have been used as unmanned radio-controlled surveillance aircraft.

A walk around a Bonanza reveals why the aeroplane has become the beloved aerial carriage of the doctor and lawyer set: quality. Beech Aircraft has always been noted for attention to fine detail, care taken in manufacture, refusal to compromise on specification regardless of cost (if you are the kind who contemplates suicide after a $100,000 loss in Las Vegas you are not the typical Beech customer, rivals say). A Bonanza, if not the Rolls-Royce of lightplanes, is surely the Lincoln Continental. The controls (still operated by that single 'throwover' wheel which the Staggerwing had, unless you pay extra for dual controls) are light, yet solid and beautifully balanced, though anyone who has flown through turbulence in a V-tail Bonanza, especially in the back seats, will tell you that the aeroplane has a nauseating tendency to 'fishtail', yawing from side to side. Bonanzaphiles claim not to notice it, and according to Beech the cause is not related to the butterfly tail. Besides, as any purist will tell you, a true Bonanza is a V-tail Bonanza, fishtailing or not.

The Bonanza is truly an aeroplane which deserves the title 'legendary'. Walter Beech, who admittedly might have been a trifle biased, described it as 'a masterpiece of engineering, an aeroplane that constitutes a modern miracle of design, a new milestone in the progress of aviation.' Immodest, perhaps, but Beech knew how to sell aeroplanes, and 13 years later *Fortune* magazine posthumously echoed his words by naming the Bonanza as one of the 100 best-designed products of modern times. The only other aeroplane in the list was the DC-3 . . .

The famous 'butterfly tail' which distinguishes the Bonanza from its contemporaries. This prototype has fabric-covered 'ruddervators'. Production aircraft have metal-skinned control surfaces.

Vickers Viscount

There's a new sound in the sky! Listen for the Viscount Whine! trumpeted London newspapers in 1953. The 'Viscount Whine' had nothing to do with complaining noblemen. It was the distinctive note of an airliner which was bringing not only a new sound but a new style to passenger travel — the Vickers Viscount, the world's first turboprop airliner to enter commercial service.

This Viscount's lineage may be traced back to the year 1943, when the British government set up a committee under the chairmanship of Lord Brabazon, the pioneer airman (and the man who first proved that old saying 'pigs might fly' by taking a squealing porker for a ride on the wing of his Voisin biplane) to determine Britain's future commercial aircraft needs.

The Brabazon Committee put forward four proposals: a large, prestigious, flag-waving, intercontinental landplane or flying boat airliner, which produced the disastrous Brabazon and Princess behemoths, neither of which ever carried anything save for a sizeable chunk of taxpayers' money; a medium-long range airliner, eventually filled by the Bristol Britannia; a fast mailplane/airliner, which became the ill-fated de Havilland Comet jetliner; and a short range airliner for services between London and European cities.

Deliberations between Committee, government and aircraft industry continued for two years, then in 1945 the latter requirement was finalized in the Brabazon IIB specification for a high-speed 24-passenger airliner. Vickers Aircraft Company's chief designer Rex Pierson duly submitted his proposal for a pressurized aircraft to be powered by a new turboprop engine called the Dart which the Rolls-Royce company was planning, with a promised power output of 850 shp. At this time the Dart did not

exist, but Rolls-Royce were beginning trials using a Gloster Meteor jet fighter powered by two Trent turbojets adapted to drive propellers. This was the world's first turboprop aircraft. Provision was also made for the proposed Vickers VC-2 to be powered by Armstrong Siddeley Mamba or Napier Naiad turboprops, though Pierson and his assistant George Edwards made no secret that they favoured the Rolls-Royce powerplant.

In March 1946 the Ministry of Supply ordered two prototypes of the aircraft, to be named Viceroy, while Vickers agreed to finance a third. Ministerial doubts and second thoughts about the choice of engine (turboprops were totally unknown at this time) complicated the early stages of the aircraft's development, and when in 1947 the government encouraged British European Airways (always plagued by government interference in its choice of aircraft) to opt for the piston-engined Airspeed Ambassador as the

Fuel efficiency, economy of operation and the legendary reliability of its whining Rolls-Royce Dart turbines have combined to give the Vickers Viscount a new lease of life. This 800-series Viscount is part of a fleet operated by the British airline Dan-Air.

mainstay of its fleet, the VC-2's future hung in jeopardy.

Only the dedication and faith of George Edwards, now chief designer for Vickers, kept work proceeding on the first prototype, now designated Type 630 and renamed Viscount after the partition of India. This prototype, powered by uprated 1,500 shp Dart turbine engines and substantially enlarged from the original proposals, made its first flight from Wisley Airfield in Surrey on 16 July 1948. 'Mutt' Summers, who had also made the Supermarine Spitfire's maiden flight, was equally impressed by the new airliner. 'It was the smoothest and best first test flight I have ever known,' he assured Edwards after the ten-minute flight.

Hedging their bets, Vickers completed the second prototype Viscount as a test-bed for two Rolls-Royce Tay pure-jet engines, but the performance of the turboprops convinced the company and the government that here was a near-perfect combination, and early in 1949 a contract was issued for a production prototype Viscount prior to a BEA order.

This Viscount 700 first flew on 28 August 1950, but one month earlier Vickers had taken the unusual step of loaning the first prototype Viscount 630 to BEA for trial commercial services. Passengers who booked a BEA flight from Northolt (then the airport for London) to Paris-Le Bourget Airport on 29 July 1950 found themselves boarding an experimental prototype, suitably licensed for the occasion, of course. During the following three weeks BEA carried 1,815 paying passengers in the aircraft on the London-Paris and London-Edinburgh routes. It was a most encouraging piece of market research which brought overwhelmingly enthusiastic passenger response. *Too* enthusiastic, perhaps. A journalist who rode on one of the flights with George Edwards noticed the hint of

above
This prototype Model 630 Viscount was loaned to British European Airways (now British Airways) in 1950 and carried a total of 1,815 passengers in three weeks' flying on London-Paris and London-Edinburgh routes.

a frown on the designer's face. 'Have you ironed all the bugs out?' he enquired. 'That's just the trouble,' replied Edwards, 'we haven't found any.'

The first order for Viscounts came from BEA in August 1950, for 20 (later increased to 26) Viscount 701s with 47-passenger cabins and powered by four 1,547 shp Dart 505 turboprops. The Viscount 701 entered service with the airline on 18 April 1953, inaugurating the world's first-ever turboprop service (the experimental trials excepted) on the London-Cyprus route via Rome and Athens.

Orders poured in for the new aircraft, from Australia, Canada, France, India, Ireland and — the most significant breakthrough in the history of British commercial aircraft — from the United States, where Capital Airlines placed an order for 60 aircraft, giving the British aircraft industry its first ever opportunity to break the stranglehold of major American aircraft manufacturers on their home ground. The Capital order paved the way for other U.S. airlines and led to sales of 147 Viscounts in North America worth £58 million. The Viscount's jet

successor, the BAC-111, has had similar success in the United States. By December 1953 Vickers had two factories building Viscounts, at Brooklands in Surrey, and at Hurn Airport near Bournemouth on England's south coast.

Public acceptance of the Viscount played a major part in its early success. That shrill 'Viscount Whine', caused by the Dart's fast-turning compressor guide vanes, provided a refreshingly quiet, vibration-free cabin environment compared to the throbbing piston engines of contemporary airliners. You could converse easily without raising your voice, and if the mood took you — at least according to the publicity handouts — you could spend your flight standing pencils and coins on edge and marvelling at the way they refused to fall over, so smooth was the new aeroplane. I doubt that coin-balancing was on the minds of many passengers who clamoured for Viscount seats, but the reduced journey times afforded by its 300-plus mph cruising speed, the comfort of a pressurized cabin which could maintain sea level pressure to 15,000 feet and a 5,500-foot cabin environment to 25,000 feet,

Compared to the prototype, this 800-series Viscount (actually a Model 833 of the former British independent airline Hunting Clan) shows the stretched fuselage incorporated in the later series aircraft.

A Viscount 806 still operated by British Airways on internal services in Britain.

and the light, airy atmosphere provided by its huge oval windows (the largest ever fitted to a commercial airliner) certainly were. It was not unusual for regular travellers between European cities to route their journeys so as to fly Viscounts all the way, even travelling from Italy to Paris via London for the benefits of turbine speed and comfort.

It was not just the passengers who appreciated the Viscount. Airlines operating the new aircraft found that their traffic (the number of travellers buying tickets, and thus the surest guide to prosperity or otherwise) increased by between 25-40 percent within weeks of taking delivery of the aircraft. Airline maintenance departments found the Dart engines wonderfully reliable and undemanding. BEA flew two specially-modified Dart-engined DC-3s for 3,000

hours to gain experience of the new engines. Vickers' cleverly-designed engine nacelles, which opened like the petals of a flower to expose the entire powerplant, made the Darts easy to work on, saving time (and thus money) during routine checks.

It was the continual refinement of Rolls-Royce's excellent powerplant, still in production for the British Aerospace HS-748 airliner and for industrial applications, which spurred the Viscount's own development. The promise of greater power from the Dart led to design studies for 'stretched' Viscounts even before the 700 series had entered service. Lest these designations confuse you, I should point out that the basic series number — 700 for example — refers to the main Viscount type, while Vickers allocated sub-type suffixes for each customer's particular

the power originally proposed by Rolls-Royce in 1945) maintained the aircraft's performance, while offering even greater economy of operation on short-haul, high-density routes.

A further variant, the Viscount 810, was developed to meet the needs of operators seeking the increased capacity of the long fuselage combined with the speed and range of the short-bodied 700-series. The Viscount 810 was powered by four 2,100 shp Dart 525 engines derated to 1,990 shp each to provide a reserve of power in 'hot-and-high' conditions, and was the last major Viscount variant. A proposed 400 mph Viscount 840, with 2,350 shp engines, was never built.

Viscount production continued, in both 700 and 800-series variants, until early in 1963. In all, 445 Viscounts were sold to 48 airlines in 40 countries, while others were delivered to military forces, governments, and to private companies and individuals as executive transports. Many are still in service, though the oldest, a 708 originally delivered to Air France in August 1953, came to an untimely end on the evening of 17 July 1980 when it ran out of fuel just short of Exeter Airport in Devon on a flight from Spain and was damaged in the ensuing forced-landing in a field. It had flown 35,109 hours. Other Viscounts still flying have amassed more than 40,000 hours, and the total time logged by the entire fleet is well into eight figures.

The Viscount was arguably the British commercial aircraft industry's finest achievement, an aeroplane which made money for its makers and operators, pleased paying customers, and which revolutionized and civilized air travel.

British Airways Viscount 806 climbing out of London-Heathrow. Square shaped passenger doors replaced the distinctive oval openings which were featured on the short-bodied 700-series Viscounts.

specification. Thus BEA's first aircraft were Viscount 701s, while Air France's were Viscount 708s, and so on.

Vickers' first plans for a 'stretched' Viscount called for a fuselage lengthened by 13 feet three inches to carry 86 passengers. Even with uprated 1,690 shp Darts this Viscount 800 would have suffered performance penalties which the company considered unacceptable, but BEA ordered 12, and a re-think in the design department came up with a compromise. The BEA Viscount 802 emerged with a fuselage just 46 inches longer than that of the 700-series, but by moving the rear pressure bulkhead further aft the effective cabin length was increased by more than nine feet, providing room for 52-71 passengers depending on the seating layout. The availability of 1,740 shp Dart 510 engines (now putting out twice

McDonnell Douglas F-4 Phantom

Outside is the noisiest, windiest, most dangerous place in the world, its air foul with kerosene fumes and steam, its atmosphere alive with tormented shrieks, piercing screams and shuddering roars punctuated by eerie klaxons and detached, metallic voices.

An aircraft carrier's deck during flying operations is a nightmare vision of Hades, a surreal kingdom presided over by Air Boss, an unseen ruler whose minions scuttle about their business on a four and a half acre slab of pitching steel made slick by the greasy residue of accumulated jet exhaust and long pencil-slash smears of melted rubber.

Their business at the moment is tending to the needs of your 25-ton fire-breathing dragon, a McDonnell-Douglas F-4B Phantom jet fighter. With the canopy latched you are removed from the noisy bustle of activity, though linked to Air Boss on his throne up in PriFli (Primary Flying Control), the 'control tower' in the carrier's island, by radio. Communication with the deck crew is by hand signal. They busy around your Phantom, looking absurdly like Mickey Mouse in their acoustic earmuffs: the men in red jerseys are refuelling and armaments crews; blues are deck crews, responsible for 'spotting' aircraft on the deck and below in the hangar; green are catapult crews; yellow are launch crews who stage manage the cat-shots, spitting four aircraft off the deck in as little as thirty seconds if need be.

41,000 pounds of thrust from two Rolls-Royce Spey 202 turbofans give this Royal Navy Phantom FG.1 (F-4K) an initial rate of climb of the order of 32,000 feet per minute.

It looks *impossible*. The distance between your Phantom and the end of the deck is 265 feet and you must have 160 knots on the airspeed indicator as you pass the bow. *Impossible.* Nothing can accelerate a 25-ton aeroplane from zero to almost 200 mph in that distance . . . except the steam catapult which can sling your Phantom aloft as easily as a kid's elastic slingshot projects a stone through your windows. Your turn now. The catapult officer waves you up to straddle the steaming slot in the carrier's deck. She's steaming into wind to give about 25 knots along the flight deck. Carrier take-offs and landings are always into wind. The deck crew attaches the heavy catapult bridle which ties the Phantom to a piston. Steam from the boiler will slam the piston along its cylinder, and you with it. The catapult officer scrawls your aircraft's weight on a board which he holds up — 51,750 pounds today — and you give him a thumbs-up to confirm. The figure is given to the catapult pressure operator below deck to ensure sufficient head of steam to get you away. *O.K.* Blast deflectors are raised behind the jetpipes of your two 17,000-pounds thrust General Electric J79 engines to protect the deck, crewmen and other aircraft from their searing heat. Aircraft handlers make a final check that all control locks and covers have been removed, that no equipment or fittings are loose, and a red-coated armaments man moves in to pull the weapons safety pins — you sit with your hands on top of your helmet while he does this — then shows them to you. Thumbs up. The cat officer checks all clear forward, raises his green flag and sweeps it round in circles, signalling you to wind up the power. Power up, bridle tensioned, all vital signs O.K. You salute the catapult officer, signifying that you accept the launch. If anything is wrong you quickly transmit *Abort* to Air Boss and firmly shake your head from side to side while keeping the power on until the steam pressure has been released and the deck crew unhook you. Salute. The catapult officer drops on one knee, brings his flag forward and down to touch the deck. *Go!* An invisible hand drags you and your Phantom to 160 knots in less than two seconds with a *6g* acceleration, not violently but with a smooth surge of brute power which never fails to thrill you and your buddy in the back seat, your Radar Intercept Officer, RIO or GIB (Guy-in-Back) for short.

A Phantom is not a pretty aeroplane, indeed one writer described it as looking like a committee-designed elephant. I would go further and say that it looks like an aeroplane designed by two committees who weren't speaking to one another. It is grotesque, ungainly, with outer wings canted up and a tail which droops down like a model made by a lad who didn't wait for the glue to set. Yet the Phantom has no rival as the most significant fighter aircraft of the 1960s and early 1970s, one which has filled needs for which it was never intended and one which has set a 20-year production record for jet fighters unequalled outside the Iron Curtain.

The Phantom started out modestly as a private venture fighter based on specifications gleaned from naval personel by company president James McDonnell. Two prototypes were ordered by the U.S. Navy in October 1954 after the original design had been revised to accommodate

Hold it there. The catapult director guides a U.S. Navy F-4J Phantom onto the catapult rail for launching.

a greater fuel load, a comprehensive weapons-control system and two crew, one to fly the aeroplane, the other to work radar and weapons systems. The first prototype, designated F4H-1 Phantom II (McDonnell had previously built a Phantom, the FH-1, in 1945) flew on 27 May 1958, and it soon became apparent that here was something very special indeed. Despite its size and apparent awkwardness the Phantom II proved to be a phenomenal performer which quickly captured a host of world records, beginning with the record for absolute altitude on 6 December 1959, when Commander Lawrence Flint Jnr. of the U.S. Navy took the YF4H-1 prototype to 98,557 feet over California's Mojave Desert. Two years later, already with a string of closed-circuit speed records under its belt, the Phantom captured the absolute world speed record at 1,606.3 mph in the hands of Lieutenant Colonel Bob Robinson of the U.S. Marine Corps. What was especially exciting

about the Phantom's record-breaking stint (it eventually captured low-level, 100-kilometre and 500-kilometre closed circuit speed records, sustained and zoom altitude records, outright speed and no fewer than eight time-to-climb records, including a flight to 30,000 metres (98,424 feet) in six minutes 11.43 seconds) was that it was a production aeroplane, not a one-off experimental type, and was clearly adaptable for a wide variety of roles.

Initially the Phantom was an exclusive U.S. Navy/Marine Corps aircraft designed for shipboard operation, but in 1961 the F-4 took part in a fly-off competition for a new tactical fighter for the United States Air Force. It proved superior to the rival Republic F-105 Thunderchief and Convair F-106 Delta Dart, and was adopted (as the F-110A, later redesignated F-4C) as the USAF's primary tactical aircraft — one of the very few occasions when air force and navy had been able to agree about anything.

The USAF had discovered that the Navy Phantom had better armament, far superior radar and higher performance than its own purpose-designed interceptors, would make a superior tactical reconnaissance aircraft and offered greater serviceability and lower maintenance demands than any of its Century-series fighters. The USAF F-4C retained the folding wings and arrestor hook of the Navy's F-4B, but incorporated new navigation and weapons systems, flying controls in the rear cockpit position, more powerful brakes and a plug-in type in-flight refuelling receptacle in place of the F-4B's boom. An unarmed RF-4C reconnaissance version was developed with oblique and panoramic cameras, infrared linescan, sideways-looking radar and electronic counter-measures (ECM) equipment.

Ironically it was to be the USAF which became the prime customer for Phantoms, with the F-4E becoming the most-produced version. This model, which first flew in August 1965, was fitted with new J79-17 engines of 17,900 pounds thrust with afterburning, miniaturized solid-state Westinghouse APQ-120 radar and a nose-mounted 20mm M61A1 rotary cannon with a 640-round ammunition pod, in addition to provision for four Sparrow missiles in under-belly recesses and up to 12,980 pounds of stores and ordnance on underwing pylons. The F-4E, 949 of which were supplied to the USAF, was also the major export version, delivered to West Germany, Greece, Iran, Israel, Turkey and Spain. Australia also used F-4Es pending delivery of General Dynamics F-111Cs, while Rolls-Royce Spey-engined F-4K and F-4M Phantoms were ordered for the British Royal Navy and Royal Air Force. The South Korean Air Force and Japanese Self Defence forces also operate Phantoms, of which more than 5,000 have been built (production by McDonnell Douglas has ended, but Mitsubishi in Japan are expected to manufacture their last F-4J in 1981),

A Royal Navy F-4K Phantom of 892 Squadron being prepared for launching from the aircraft carrier H.M.S. *Ark Royal*. Note the extended nosewheel leg which raises the Phantom to the correct take-off altitude on the catapult.

including 1,264 for the U.S. Navy and Marine Corps and 2,650 for the USAF.

Perhaps half the Phantoms built have actually seen combat, in either the Vietnam or Middle East wars. Like the F-86 Sabres in Korea, Phantoms have had an edge in air-to-air combat because of the superiority of their pilot training. Though the elderly MiG-17s used by the North Vietnamese early in the war were clearly no match for the Phantoms, the MiG-21 could outmanoeuvre F-4s prior to the E models, which were fitted with leading edge slats after 1972, simply by pulling tight turns which the Phantom could not follow. The lack of an internal gun on models before F-4E was also a handicap for dogfighting. Colonel Robin Olds, a World War II veteran with 13 kills to his credit, who destroyed four MiGs during a combat tour in South East Asia flying F-4s, noted later in the Grumman company's house magazine *Horizons*: 'Air-to-air missiles gave our fighters a tremendous capability relative to the

Pilot's station (front seat) of a Phantom with Westinghouse APQ-120 multi-mode radar display screen at top centre.

MiG-17, which carried only cannons and rockets. But fighting a MiG with a gunless F-4 is like fighting a guy with a dagger when he's got a sword, or maybe vice-versa. A fighter without a gun, which is the most versatile air-to-air weapon, is like an airplane without a wing. Five or six times, when I had fired all my missiles, I might have been able to hit a MiG if I'd had cannon, because I was so close his motion was stopped in my gunsight.'

The General Electric M-61 Vulcan cannon fitted to the F-4E had a 6,000 rounds per minute rate of fire, more than adequate to bring down a MiG with a one-second burst. Lieutenant Randall 'Duke' Cunningham, first American pilot to become a five-victory ace over Vietnam (shared with his RIO Lieutenant William 'Willie' Driscoll) flew Navy Phantoms, and described his three-kill battle with MiG-17's during an airstrike against railway yards near Hanoi on 10 May 1972 thus: 'I bored in on the '17 head on. Suddenly his whole nose lit up like a Christmas tree! . . . This guy was really spitting out the 23mm and 37mm. I pulled hard, up in the vertical, figuring that the MiG would keep right on going for home. I looked back . . . and there was the MiG. He couldn't have been more than thirty feet away . . . I could see the pilot clearly, leather helmet, goggles, scarf . . . we were both going straight up . . . in the vertical, [when] an idea came to me . . . I went to idle and speed brakes . . . and he shot out in front of me! I think it really surprised him, being out in front of me for the first time. Anyway, we're both going straight up and losing speed fast. I was down to 150 knots and I knew I was going to have to go to full burner to hold it. I did, and we both pitched over the top. As he came over I used rudder to get the airplane to turn to his belly side . . . He pitched over the top and started straight down. I went after him and though I didn't think the Sidewinder would guide straight down with all the heat of the ground to look at [the Sidewinder is a heat-seeking missile which homes in on the target's jet pipe] I squeezed one off anyway. The missile came off the rail and went to his airplane. There was just a little flash, and I thought, ''God, it missed him!'' I started to fire my last Sidewinder and suddenly a big flash of flame and black smoke erupted from his airplane. He didn't seem to go out of control but flew straight down into the ground.'

But the Phantom's real value in Vietnam was not as a dogfighter so much as a 'can-do' master of all trades which excelled in every unlikely role demanded of it and continues to do so with the air arms of ten nations. Seldom, if ever, in the history of military aviation have so many talents been combined in one airframe.

Mission accomplished. One hour forty minutes since the catapult spat your Phantom off the deck, and now you are orbiting the ship at 2,500 feet, number three to land. The lead ship in your formation starts down, passing along the ship's starboard side, then breaking left to set up the downwind leg for landing. The other Phantoms will follow at precise 50-second separations, curving in towards the carrier to pick up the Visual Approach Slope Indicator which gives them a visual cue to the correct approach attitude. Three quarters of a mile out you curve in to line up with the deck, foreshortened until it seems no bigger than a tennis court. You radio the Landing Signal Officer (LSO) that you have aquired the landing sight, a bright white ball which you must keep in the middle of a row of green lights. The LSO will be monitoring your landing through an optical sight and cueing you on his short range radio. The aim is to trap the number three arrester cable. Nice steady constant rate descent, looking good, ball in the centre, airspeed 145 knots, but the captain's giving you about 25 knots of wind along the deck, so you will touchdown at 120 with a sink rate of about 20 feet per second. Still looking good, but the LSO will have the final say. If he is not happy with your approach he will tell you to go around again, and you *must*, if necessary breaking off and climbing up to take on more fuel from the tanker orbiting high above the carrier. Not this time though. Deck coming up, full military power as you touch down in case the arrestor hook misses all the wires and you have to go around. The engines take time to spool up, so you must apply full power on *every* landing just in case, or you could go over the side. Every landing is videotaped. Pilots who go to full power a little late, or are too enthusiastic and go through the gate into full afterburner may be sure their sins will find them out. Perfect, right on the money. Number three wire snags your hook as you slam onto the deck, reels out, seeming to stretch like an elastic band, and draws you to a smooth halt in one hundred yards. The deck crew signal 'hook free', and you roll forward again, folding the Phantom's outer wing panels and clearing the landing area for the next aircraft, already turning onto his final approach. Air Boss will be pleased with that one.

above
Cat shot. From zero to 160 knots in two seconds, a U.S. Navy F-4J Phantom crosses the bow of U.S.S. *Constellation* after a catapult launch.

left
A 25-ton fighter is an unlikely aerobatic mount, but Phantoms were used during the 1970s by both the USAF Thunderbirds and (seen here) US Navy Blue Angels formation display teams. Fuel economy measures have forced both teams to switch to smaller aircraft, the Thunderbirds to Northrop T-38s, the Angels to Douglas A-4 Skyhawks.

Cessna 172 Skyhawk

Every once in a while, without flourish or fanfare, comes a product so perfectly attuned to the market that it outlives every brash newcomer to become an ageless institution. The Model T Ford and Volkswagen Beetle spring to mind. And the Douglas DC-3 and Piper Cub. But top of my list would be the Cessna 172, which has sold in greater numbers than any other light aeroplane and with total production now running at more than 30,000 draws ever closer to becoming the world's most-produced aircraft of any kind (the title holders, in case you should want to win bets from your friends, are: Messerschmitt Bf109 series, 35,000; Yakovlev YAK-1/9 series, 37,000; and

Ilyushin IL-2/IL-10 Stormovik series, top at 41,000).

We left Clyde Cessna, you will recall, when he broke his partnership with Walter Beech to set up his own business in Wichita. During the post-Depression years of the mid 1930s Cessna Aircraft Company gained a reputation as a manufacturer of efficient high-wing monoplanes under the guiding hand of Cessna's nephew Dwayne Wallace, who took over as plant manager and chief engineer of the company in 1934, finally retiring in 1975. But Cessna was still a low-volume producer. It was not until the war in Europe broke out, and Cessna's T-50 twin-engine aircraft filled a gap as a trainer for the Empire Air Training Programme in Canada that the company was finally established as one of America's 'big three' manufacturers of light aircraft along with Beech and Piper, a triumvirate which still dominates the private aeroplane market worldwide.

After the war Cessna concentrated on the anticipated plane-in-every-garage boom (which never materialized) with the two-seat 85 hp Models 120 and 140, and the 145 hp four-seat Model 170. The line was expanded later to include the radial-engined 190 and 195, which were scaled-up all-metal versions of the pre-war Airmaster series, and the 180, a rugged four-seat tailwheel design which

This view of a current model Cessna Skyhawk shows the evolution of the world's most popular lightplane when compared to the photograph of the original Cessna 170 on page 148.

The Cessna 170 was Cessna's first postwar four-seater. This one is an early model with fabric-covered parallel-chord wings, later replaced with all-metal semi-tapered surfaces.

remains in production and is a favourite of farmers, bush pilots and other work-aday fliers who appreciate its load-hauling capability and resilient airframe.

The Cessna 170 became the best-selling model in the company's line (more than 5,000 were built), and in 1955 Cessna introduced a new four-seater intended to supplement rather than replace the earlier machine. The Model 172 had an airframe similar to the 170's but with the square-cut tail surfaces of the 180 and — an innovation for Cessna — a tricycle undercarriage promising easier ground handling than the tailwheel landing gear which earned the 170 a reputation as a real pilot's aeroplane (a euphemism meaning tricky to handle) on narrow runways in crosswinds. Those 'real pilots' were quick to deride the 172's 'training wheel' on the nose, dismissing it as a short-lived novelty.

They were very soon proven wrong. In its first year of production the Cessna 172 outsold the 170 seven to one; in its second year the ratio went up to twelve to one and by 1957 the 170 was ousted from the Cessna range entirely.

The reason for the 172's instant popu-larity is difficult to pinpoint. Not speed, since the added drag of the nosewheel actually made it a few miles per hour slower than the contemporary Cessna 170B. But it certainly looked 'modern', and was more likely to appeal to a pilot who wanted an aeroplane which he could handle on the ground as he might his car rather than one which would sometimes behave like a rudderless yacht when the wind was wrong. The 172 was intended to bridge the generation gap between

pre-war pilots trained on cantankerous biplanes and tricky taildraggers and a new breed of young fliers seeking a business or pleasure aircraft which did not demand professional skills. Purists scoff at this 'automobile of the air' approach to marketing, but manufacturers laugh only on the way to the bank.

The earliest Cessna 172s were basic machines which came with one choice of overall colour: unpainted aluminium, though an accent stripe was standard. The first major change to the aircraft came with the 1960 model year (like car manufacturers the major lightplane companies announce 'new' models each autumn, though as often as not only detail fittings and paint scheme are changed). Gone was the square, upright vertical fin in favour of a rakish swept-back stabilizer which befitted the new decade but was influenced more by Cessna's marketing department than their aerodynamicists. A name was given to the aeroplane: Skyhawk, though it was and is best known the world over as the One-Seventy-Two. Three years later came a new fuselage, cut down aft of the cabin to incorporate rear windows (*Omnivision* in Cessna-speak) which improved visibility to the rear and gave the cabin a roomier and more airy ambiance. At the same time a production line was set up at Reims, France, to feed a voracious European market. Some years before, Cessna had offered the British de Haviland company a licence production agreement, but were turned down, killing off what was perhaps the last

chance to re-establish the once buoyant British light aircraft industry, now sadly all but extinct. More major changes followed in 1968 when Cessna substituted a 150 hp Lycoming 'Blue Streak' engine for the long-serving Continental, and also introduced a new model called the 177 Cardinal which was a slick sports-saloon to the 172's family sedan. Few observers doubted that, as the 172 had to the 170, the Cardinal would soon oust the older machine from the Wichita production lines, but it never did and is now discontinued, while the 172 is still being manufactured.

One might be forgiven for thinking that the world's best selling lightplane would be a product of inspired design, of radical innovation, but the Cessna 172 is the very antithesis of such a notion. Rather, it is a basically sound product which has been steadily improved piecemeal — a little styling change here, a touch of aerodynamic refinement there — into a paragon of reliability and dependability (except for those 6,500 or so 1977-80 models which had troublesome 160 hp Lycoming 0-320-H engines, now replaced in 1981 models). A new wing leading edge was added in 1973 to improve the 172's already excellent low-

A 'straight-tail' Cessna 172, little more than a 170B with squared-off tail surfaces and tricycle undercarriage, pictured in 1956.

Instrument panel and cabin interior of a current model Cessna Skyhawk.

formers which excels in no particular field but which is in sporting terms a good all-rounder with no brilliant character-istics, but no diabolical ones either. A One-Seventy-Two is a willing work-horse, comfortable as an old shoe, and instantly familiar to any pilot who learns to fly in its smaller brother (or sister if you think of aeroplanes as female), the Cessna 150, which is the world's most popular training aeroplane. What more natural than the step up to the four-seater? Wise lightplane manufacturers are ever mind-ful of the need for product continuity to encourage brand-loyalty, and for no valid reason a pilot who learns to fly on a Cessna tends to stick with Cessnas, just as one who learns in a low-wing aero-plane will likely have a preference for aircraft whose wings are at his feet rather than above his head.

Let's go for a flight in this ubiquitous lightplane. The 1981 Skyhawk II is a far cry from that 'training wheel 170' of 1955: there's even an optional air conditioner. In the older 172s you either sweltered on the ground or cracked open a door. The doors in fact, have changed least, big and wide, making entry and exit easy even for back-seat passengers, and the aeroplane is cleared for flight with the doors removed, making it a popular mount for aerial cameramen. A baggage compart-ment behind the rear seats takes 120 lbs of luggage. Cabin trim is of the family car rather than the limousine variety, but the colour-toned furnishings are comfortable and functional.

Fuel for the 160 hp Lycoming engine is fed from two wing tanks by that most reliable device, gravity, though there is also an electric fuel pump. The engine starts readily and by lightplane stand-ards, is fairly quiet. The 172's nosewheel is linked to the rudder pedals and the new wide-track landing gear makes ground-handling a pleasure (this is the auto-mobile of the air remember). Given its head a 172 will take-off almost by itself, indeed a flying instructor friend of mine used to prove the point by sitting with his arms folded during the take-off roll while his students would sit twitching nerv-ously in the left seat. He claims that he once flew an entire cross-country trip without touching the aircraft's control wheel, using trimmer, rudder pedals and throttle to direct his flight, just to prove that even jammed controls would not necessarily be catastrophic in the benign 172.

The Skyhawk hardly sparkles, per-formance-wise. A modest increase in horsepower has boosted rate of climb

speed handling; an aerodynamic clean-up the following year added a knot or two in cruise speed; tapered steel tube landing gear legs replaced the original spring-steel units for better ground handling and ride: subtle improvements which little by little helped make a good aeroplane better. More power was offered in the 1977 Hawk XP, which had a 195 hp engine driving a constant speed propeller (a similar version known as the Reims Rocket had been manufactured in France for some time), and in 1979 Cessna introduced the ultimate refinement of the basic 172 design, a retractable under-carriage model with a 180 hp engine called the Cutlass RG.

But it is the plain no-frills Cessna 172 which continues to be the best seller and, like the DC-3, to outlive its intended successors. Why? I suppose because it is one of those middle-of-the-road per-

French-built Reims-Cessna F172 Skyhawk, licence-built for the European market.

from about 550 feet per minute in the older examples to 770 feet per minute in the 1981 model, but no amount of persuasion will get much more than 120 knots true airspeed from the aeroplane. That is not so bad. True, other aeroplanes go faster on the same horsepower, or carry more payload, and some of them look prettier, but few combine all of the 172's charms, and even with a stiff headwind the Cessna will return a better journey time point-to-point than you could hope to achieve by road unless you happen to own a Turbo Porsche and are immune to radar speed traps.

Slow speed is perhaps the 172's forte. It has huge 'barn door' Fowler flaps which extend outwards first to increase wing area and create more lift, then droop to add drag. The latest models have flaps which droop only 30 degrees; previous 172's flaps went down 40 degrees for real action-stopping drag, but never try to climb away from an abandoned landing with those great boards hanging full-out; the 172 just will not climb that way. With flaps up the 172 stalls at about 40 knots; ten degrees of flap reduces the stalling speed to around 35 knots; with full flap (and a lot of power to counter the drag) it seems to keep on flying for ever, with the airspeed indicator hovering indecisively at the very bottom of its arc. The slow-flight characteristics of the 172 make it easy to land and have contributed to an excellent safety record in stall-spin accidents, which are among the most common lightplane crashes. The 172 also has an excellent reliability record apart from that engine hiccup we mentioned earlier. Some years ago Cessna borrowed a privately-owned 172 which had logged over 12,000 flying hours (equivalent to about 18 months in the air). They inspected every part of the aeroplane but could find no major components showing signs of wear or needing replacement.

How best to sum up the 172, which has had the greatest influence on post-war lightplane travel? Safe, forgiving, dependable, an 'average' aeroplane (aren't most people 'average'?), comfortingly predictable not in a boring sense but in the way that your favourite arm-chair or bar is predictable. That's why more than 30,000 people have bought them.

British Aerospace Harrier

Great vortices of dust obliterate the source of the noise as it rises to an ear-shattering, nerve-protesting crescendo. From a bubbling cauldron of exhaust gases a small jet fighter rises vertically, poised precariously on a column of air like a table-tennis ball at a fairground shooting gallery. It pirouettes around, then as if fatally stricken, teeters back onto its tail, nose rising to an impossible angle until you can hardly bear to watch, for it must surely tumble from its invisible perch and fall back explosively to the ground. But no. As the nose rises even more, to what seems like a near-vertical angle, sitting on its tail, the jet begins a slow climb, moving almost imperceptibly upwards with that ponderous nail-biting hesitancy of the Apollo moonshots leaving the launch pad, when thrust and gravity hold equal sway, and finally it rockets away through the cloud cover while ten thousand spectators let go

simultaneously a breath held much too long.

Thus test pilot John Farley performs his favourite airshow party-piece in the British Aerospace Harrier, popularly known as the 'Jump Jet', for it is the western world's only operational Vertical Take-Off and Landing (VTOL) jet fighter.

Why VTOL? Because of the vulnerability of front-line airfields to enemy attack. All the aircraft and pilots in the world are worthless if the runways from which they operate are destroyed or put out of service, as many Royal Air Force stations were during the Battle of Britain. An aircraft which can take off and land vertically without need of conventional runways can turn any clearing, any road into an airfield, offering great tactical flexibility and a valuable element of surprise.

In the early 1950s the VTOL fighter concept was explored in the United States

Royal Air Force Harrier GR.1s which first entered service in 1969. These aircraft have now been updated with more powerful Pegasus 103 engines of 21,500 pounds thrust and re-designated Harrier GR.3.

with a pair of turboprop-engined prototypes — incongruously named Pogo and Salmon — which were supposed to auger their way into the sky while hanging on their giant contra-rotating propellers, and with a tiny jet which stood on its tail for take-off, but neither scheme was practicable.

The availability of high thrust/weight-ratio jet engines also inspired some weird VTOL craft in Britain, including the Rolls-Royce Thrust-Measuring Rig, beloved by the popular press as the *Flying Bedstead,* and Hawker Aircraft's Sydney Camm, the Hurricane man, gathered together a design team to turn the data gathered from research into a practical VTOL combat aircraft.

Central to the project was the revolutionary new BS.53 turbofan engine being developed by Doctor Stanley Hooker of Bristol Siddeley Engines (now Rolls-Royce). Hooker and Camm got together in 1957. Instead of opting for the tail-sitting stance or the use of separate lift and thrust engines as other experimenters had, they proposed to use a single engine to lift the aircraft vertically from the ground and to propel it after transitioning to horizontal flight, using pivoting exhaust nozzles to direct the engine's thrust wherever it was needed.

The first prototype of Camm's P.1127 design made its maiden flight (strictly speaking its maiden hover) on 21 October 1960. Within a year the P.1127 had achieved the most difficult part of the VTOL operation — transitioning from vertical to horizontal flight. A developed version of the prototype called the Kestrel F(GA)1 was evaluated by a tripartite squadron made up of pilots from the services of Britain, West Germany and the United States in 1965, and the production-standard Harrier GR.1 ground-attack/reconnaissance fighter entered service with the Royal Air Force on 1

April 1969. The U.S. Marine Corps also operates the Harrier as the AV-8A, as does the Spanish Navy, with whom it is known as Matador. (The Spanish aircraft were supplied via the United States against the wishes of the British Government, which has been wary of encouraging exports of the Harrier, thus seriously hampering sales of a unique and much sought-after aircraft). A naval

Sea Harrier FRS.1s breaking right during a training sortie from the Royal Naval Air Station at Yeovilton, Somerset.

Sea Harrier FRS.1 version is now operational with the British Royal Navy, providing that service's only fixed-wing air cover from new-generation 'Harrier Carrier' through-deck Command cruisers.

The Camm/Hooker Vectorable Thrust concept is the heart of the Harrier and the key to its amazing versatility. Thrust from the 21,500-pound Rolls-Royce Pegasus turbofan is exhausted through four nozzles which are mechanically linked so that separate jets can be swivelled simultaneously from the fully aft position (as on a conventional jet engine) to a position slightly forward of the vertical, some 60 percent of total thrust being discharged from the low pressure compressor through the front pair of nozzles while high-pressure turbine exhaust gas is discharged through the rear pair. Control of the engine is effected with a conventional throttle which adjusts engine speed and thus the *length* of the vectored thrust, while a second nozzle lever controls the *direction* of the thrust vector, swivelling the nozzles by means of a Nozzle Actuation System which uses an air motor driven by engine compressor air and a system of shafts, bevel gears and chains to orientate the nozzles.

British Aerospace's chief test pilot John Farley says the Harrier is easy to fly, adding, disarmingly, 'It is also very easy to crash.' A VTOL take-off calls for some

dexterity. Remember that at zero airspeed the Harrier's conventional control surfaces — ailerons, elevators and rudder — which rely on airflow for effectiveness, are worthless, so a supplementary Reaction Control System is installed which takes bleed air from the Pegasus engine's compressor and feeds it to reaction control valves at each wingtip, nose and tail. These valves operate in much the same way as the 'puffers' fitted to orbiting spacecraft, exerting a reaction force to move the aeroplane in the desired direction. The valves are linked to the Harrier's control column, operating in the natural sense (easing the stick back gives a downward 'puff', raising the aircraft's nose) and are automatically brought into operation whenever the nozzles are vectored beyond 20 degrees from the horizontal-flight position. The reaction control system is very effective and carefully designed to provide the pilot with a progressive 'feel' just as the Harrier's conventional controls do, but it has limitations in the degree of correction which the 'puffers' can handle without depriving the hard-working engine of thrust, particularly in the roll and yaw axes. An unwitting yaw or sideslip can very easily cause the Harrier to roll beyond the reaction valves' corrective powers and the aeroplane effectively 'falls off' its supporting column of air and crashes back to earth. When things go wrong in the Harrier they go wrong very quickly and very close to the ground. Fortunately the aircraft is equipped with a zero-zero Martin Baker ejector seat which can punch you out safely to 300 feet even when the machine is stationary on the ground.

For a standard (not that there is anything standard about it) VTOL departure the throttle is set at 55 percent rpm with the nozzles fully aft, then the nozzle lever is brought forward to the pre-set VTO stop, swivelling the nozzles to 80 degrees relative to the engine, which equates to 88 degrees relative to the ground, while the throttle is advanced to full power and away she goes. Contrary to popular myth the Harrier does not scorch grass or melt tarmac with hot exhaust during VTOL operations. The front-nozzle exhaust gases are at temperatures around 100 degrees Centigrade, while the rear nozzles exhaust is about 670 degrees Centigrade, but as the take-off is accomplished so smartly there is little time for the heat to transfer to the underlying surface. The standard Harrier 'airfield' at unprepared sites is a 70-foot square aluminium mat, and even on wooden

decks of ships no damage has been detected during Harrier operations. The transition from jet-borne to wing-borne flight is accomplished by gradually rotating the nozzles aft and accelerating away. The total time needed for VTO and transition to wingborne flight is typically around 20 seconds and takes less than 100 pounds of fuel. The reverse transition, from wingborne flight to the hover for a Vertical Landing, is one of the key manoeuvres in Harrier flying. A typical landing approach begins in conventional forward flight with the airspeed at 200 knots, airbrake, flaps and landing gear lowered, while the nozzles are slowly rotated downwards, decelerating the aircraft until it becomes partially jetborne at 100 knots, at which point the sink rate is controlled with the throttle and the Harrier brought to the hover at about 50 feet, ready to be lowered onto the ground by tiny throttle adjustments. Vertical landing has many advantages in tactical deployment: no runway is needed, even tall trees are no problem if a clearing can be made; wind direction is of little importance; accurate approach paths need not be flown; and poor weather need not curtail operations.

In operational service with the RAF, Harriers are usually recovered by vertical landing, but vertical take-offs are rarely used because the aircraft is weight-limited in VTOL mode and cannot lift a full load of fuel and weaponry, though it can VTO with about 50 percent of its maximum disposable load. For missions where vertical take-off is not essential the Short Take-Off (STO) technique, with the nozzles pointing aft, until the Harrier reaches anything from 50-130 knots depending on aircraft weight and ambient air temperatures, then rotating the nozzles downwards to the pre-set STO stop to lift the aircraft off on a combination of wing lift and engine thrust for the normal transition to fully-wingborne flight. A typical Harrier STO, with the nozzles vectored to 50 degrees down at the appropriate groundspeed, involves a five to seven second ground roll and a run of about 200 yards. In STO mode every extra foot of ground run permits an additional six pounds of fuel or weapons to be carried, and every extra knot of wind permits an additional 66 pounds of payload.

The Ski-Jump invented by Royal Navy Lieutenant Commander Doug Taylor and

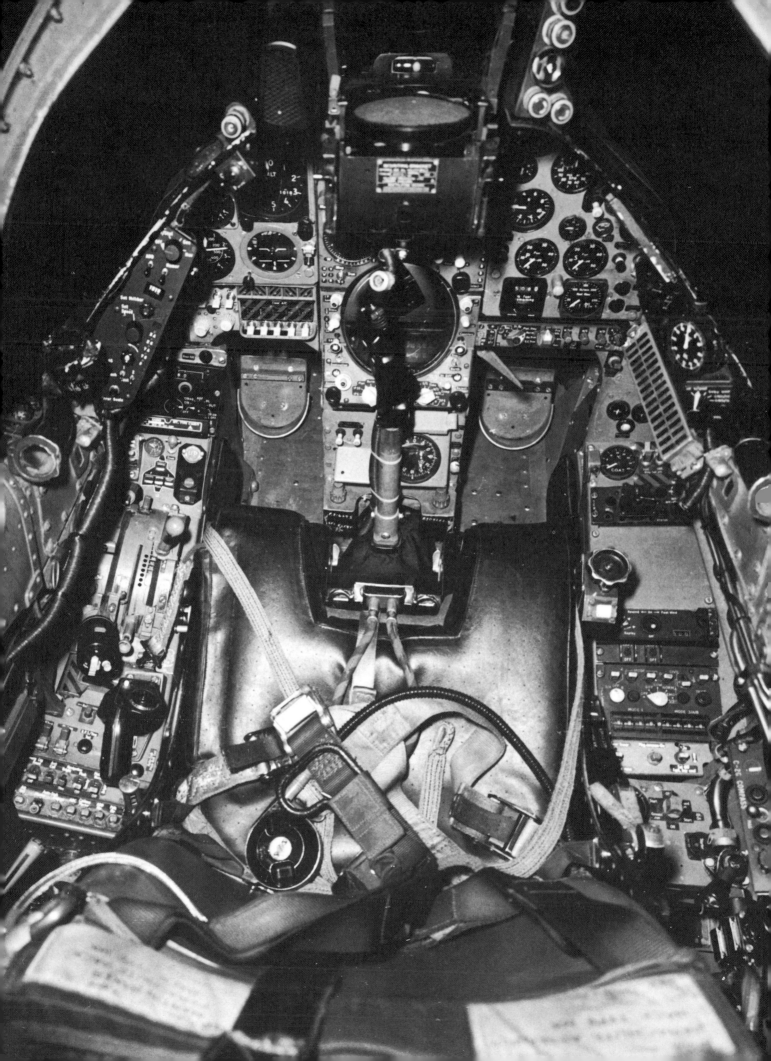

now installed on the latest British command cruisers *Invincible*, *Illustrious* and *Ark Royal* further exploits the Harrier's STO capability (which is unique — the Soviet YAK-36 Forger can only operate in VTO mode). Taylor discovered that an upward sloping ramp angled between six and twenty degrees significantly decreased the ground roll needed to launch a Harrier performing a Short Take-Off, while offering valuable payload benefits. With a 15-degree 'ski-jump', for example, a Harrier can carry an additional 3,000 pounds of fuel or underwing ordnance and get off with a ground roll of 600 feet. Comparable 'flat' STO performance, *without* the additional payload, would require a 1,200 foot run. The ski-jump, for which Lieutenant-Commander Taylor received a £25,000 honararium, is applicable to both sea and land operations, and is, according to British Aerospace's Harrier Marketing Director John Fozard, 'a great leap [!] for tactical air power.'

But then great leaps are part of the the Harrier's stock in trade, as is a manoeuvre quite unique to this aircraft's repertoire: Vectoring In Forward Flight, or VIFFing, which gives the Harrier a tactical advantage over aircraft of superior performance. The technique was developed by the U.S. Marine Corps, whose AV-8As carry missiles for air-to-air combat. The RAF's, used primarily in ground attack

roles, do not. VIFFing involves the use of the full range of thrust vectors in wingborne flight, and requires strengthening of the exhaust nozzles to avoid overstressing. Imagine a Harrier being pursued by a faster attacker at, say, 500 knots. By moving his nozzle control lever rapidly forward, rotating the nozzles to the vertical, the Harrier pilot can decelerate his aircraft at a rate of 30 knots per second, seemingly stopping in midair (a typical aerodynamic airbrake on a jet fighter decelerates it at five knots per second) while the pursuer overshoots and becomes the pursued. Rapid vectoring can decelerate and accelerate the Harrier in an instant. The same technique can be used to slow the aircraft in steep dives for unrivalled accuracy in weapons-delivery on ground targets, and a VIFFing turn, with nozzles rotated 50 degrees down, reduces the Harrier's turning radius by 50 percent.

The Harrier is arguably the most exciting flying machine yet devised, certainly the most versatile, with a speed range from a minus quantity (it can fly backwards) to transonic. Small wonder that John Farley's moon-shot lift-off (accomplished by rotating the aircraft and nozzles so that the thrust is always pointing at the ground) never fails to win a round of applause at airshows, even from the most blasé spectators. And in the Harrier, he can even take a bow . . .

A Sea Harrier FRS.1 operating in VTOL mode from the helicopter platform of the Royal Fleet Auxiliary tanker RFA *Olwen*, emphasizing the extraordinary flexibility of the aircraft.

opposite
A Harrier cockpit.

General Dynamics F-111

It comes at you faster than a bullet, hugging the ground, following its every contour like a supersonic roller coaster, transformed in an instant from a distant speck into a sinister lizard-camouflaged dart which is on you and gone before you can think, leaving you gaping, open-mouthed, stunned at its suddenness . . . or dead, according to whether you are friend or enemy.

The General Dynamics F-111E, known (notorious, indeed) in the early 1960s as TFX, which really stood for Tactical Fighter Experimental but is noted by one sceptical observer as Terrible (expletive deleted) Experience, is a child of controversy, the product of an acrimonious forced marriage of air force and navy requirements which scandalized the Pentagon and earned the aeroplane a reputation as an expensive lemon which tried to do everything and succeeded in doing nothing very well.

A talk with any F-111 pilot — they call the aircraft 'Aardvark' — will leave you with a very different and more accurate

impression: 'There's only one word that describes the F-111 in a nutshell. That word is unique. When a weapon system has a unique capability it becomes a priceless machine. Unique doesn't mean just higher, faster and farther than some previous model. It means opening a combat arena where you have superiority because you are the only one operating there.'

How is the F-111 unique? It has the speed and manoeuvrability of a fighter; the payload of a bomber; range sufficient to cross oceans on internal fuel only. It can fly at tree-top height in all weather, or at 60,000 feet. It can dogfight, bomb or strafe ground targets, launch conventional or nuclear weapons, fly at more than twice the speed of sound at high altitude or go supersonic at sea level.

There is more. The F-111 was the first production aircraft to employ variable geometry — 'swing wings'; the first to have afterburning turbofan engines; the first tactical figther-bomber to weigh more than 50 tons; the first to have the capability to bomb unseen targets by night or in cloud with a certainty of being able to hit a 50-yard area, every time.

The F-111 is an extraordinary aeroplane. It is huge, as long as a World War II B-17 Flying Fortress. Its wings pivot on eight-and-a-half inch steel pins, swinging from their fully extended position of 16 degrees sweepback to 72.5 degrees, transforming the aircraft from a gawky ungainly bird to a fair representation of a schoolboy's paper dart. Variable geometry has been with us since 1911 and has been toyed with by numerous experimenters ever since, but it was not until 1959 that engineers at the National Aeronautics and Space Administration's Langley Research Center discovered the key to success. They adopted separate pivots for each wing as opposed to the single pivot used in previous experiments. The pivotal points could therefore be moved out from the aircraft's centreline, avoiding the trim and stability problems caused by a shifting of the aircraft's centre of lift as the wings sweep

A USAF F-111F cruising high over the Rocky Mountains.

F-111 production line at General Dynamics Corporation's Fort Worth, Texas, facility.

through their range. An F-111 pilot can effectively 'redesign' his aircraft in flight, configuring the wing for any flight regime: fully extended for take-off, landing and slow flight, at full sweepback while supersonic. The wing is fitted with full span slats and flaps which give the F-111 remarkable short-field capability. It can take off or land even from rough unprepared airstrips in less than 3,000 feet (ground-rolls of less than 2,000 feet have been achieved), while the variable geometry wings are the key to its versatility in combining bomber payloads and range with fighter performance.

How is it to fly? That word unique comes to mind again. The two-crew pressurized cockpit, unusually for a fighter-bomber arranged in side-by-side configuration, has no ejector seats, no parachutes. It is part of a complete nose module which can be blasted away from the rest of the airframe by a shaped plastic explosive charge which shears the entire front end of the aircraft away. The module, complete with crew, is rocketted 350-2,000 feet high, depending on the aircraft's airspeed at the time of the crew departure, and descends to earth on an Apollo-sized parachute dispensing radar reflecting metallic 'chaff' en route so that the crew's descent may be tracked by ground radar for a speedy pick-up. A portion of the wingroot gives the module stability in 'flight' (so good that a test

crew forced to bail out of an early F-111 prototype reputedly opened the cockpit windows and leaned out to enjoy the view on the way down), while inflated bags cushion the shock of meeting the earth, or right the module if a landing is made on water, in which case the aircraft's now-redundant control column serves as a bilge pump (forward movement) or as an air pump (backward movement) to keep the flotation bags topped up. On the few occasions when the escape module has needed to be used (F-111's have an enviable safety record in the USAF inventory: only six were lost in over 4,000 combat missions in Vietnam) it has worked impeccably.

Every part of the F-111 which is not filled with engines or weapons systems is full of fuel: a huge tank behind the crew module, saddle tanks atop the twin Pratt & Whitney TF30-P-3 turbofan engines, even a tank in the vertical fin and in the wing-box which houses the variable geometry mechanism, and of course provision beneath the wings for external tanks whose pylons are engineered to compensate automatically for wing-sweep and to keep droptanks and underwing ordnance aligned with the aircraft's centreline. With internal fuel only, an F-111E, which forms the vanguard of the USAF's strike capability in Europe, weighs 92,500 pounds (a Phantom with full internal fuel and three external tanks weighs some

A fine plan view of an F-111A with wings at the minimum sweep (16 degrees) angle. At maximum sweep the wing trailing edge aligns with the leading edges of the horizontal stabilizers.

52,500 pounds) and can deploy from the United States to British and European bases or fly across America nonstop without air-to-air refuelling. With inflight refuelling the F-111's operational range becomes more a matter of crew endurance than aircraft limitation.

Much of the credit for the F-111's long range is due to the fuel efficiency of its TF30 turbofans at cruise power settings. With full afterburner the F-111E's TF30-P-3s are rated at 18,500 pounds static thrust each. Not only did these engines offer afterburning (the injection of raw fuel into the aft end of one of the engine's combustion chambers to increase thrust) for the first time on a turbofan engine, but the afterburner thrust can be modulated. Hitherto afterburner thrust was either on or off, all or nothing. On the TF30 the pilot can vary the afterburner thrust smoothly over its entire range, and an automatically adjusting 'spike' in each air intake varies the air inlet geometry, controlling the inlet shock-wave pattern and maintaining a regular flow of air to the engines for optimum performance throughout the aircraft's wide speed range. How wide? The F-111E stalls at around 95 knots, incredibly slow for such a heavy, high-performance aircraft. Its maximum speed is not public knowledge, but devoid of external stores is certainly in excess of Mach 2.5 (1,640 mph) at altitude, and Mach 1.2 (800 mph) at sea level.

The F-111E is very much a 'left-hand' aeroplane. The pilot sits on the left, his Weapons Systems Officer (WSO or Wizzo) on the right, and the pilot's left hand must operate two throttles, flap, slat and speedbrake controls, landing gear retraction and the wing sweep, which is controlled by a sliding handle operating in the natural sense (forward to open out the wings, back for maximum sweep) which gives full travel over the entire range in 15 seconds.

Taxying the beast needs care, for the long proboscis of the Aardvark extends way ahead of the cockpit, and the narrow long stroke main undercarriage legs and fat tyres which cushion the hardest of slam 'em down landings can induce the F-111 to list sharply if too tight a turn is attempted. Even the undercarriage is unique, with mainwheels mounted on a single trunnion which ensures that both legs retract simultaneously and provides the added safety and reliability of having but a single retraction mechanism. The forward main gear door doubles as a speedbrake. While taxying, jets of air from underbelly nozzles blast debris from the taxiway to prevent it being sucked into the air intakes and causing foreign object damage to the engines — not vital on well-maintained airfields but essential for the F-111's rough-strip operations.

Throttles forward, past the detent which marks the start of afterburner

Imposing choice of stores for the F-111, pictured here with variable-geometry wings at maximum sweepback.

range. Acceleration is brisk for a 50-ton aeroplane. Rotate the nose at 140 knots and things get busy: flaps up at 180 knots; slats in at 250 knots, then as speed increases and the extra lift afforded by the fully-extended wings begins to convert to drag they must be brought back to the first intermediate position, 26 degrees, then to 54 degrees to go transonic, fully back at Mach 1.7 and above, where maximum speed is limited only by the need to keep the aircraft's skin temperatures within limits to avoid structural damage. In cruise flight the F-111 has the stability of an airliner, though fingertip pressure will roll it at Mach 2. At wing sweep angles of 45 degrees or less, roll control is by spoilers on the wings which give instantaneous response at a rate of 170 degrees per second, the spoiler on the downgoing wing first deploying fully to

overcome its inertia, then adjusting to maintain the roll rate. At greater sweep angles the rear stabilizers/elevons operate differentially to roll the aircraft. The flight control system uses electronic sensors and computers to monitor the aircraft's inflight motion, automatically compensating for deviations with direct commands to the control surfaces, so that, for example, pitch, roll or yaw commands will be made to counteract strong gusts or turbulence before the pilot senses the need for control inputs, and the system is triplicated. The failure of one circuit, or a faulty response, is automatically ignored by the other two who 'outvote' it.

But it is the F-111's navigation and weapons delivery systems which make it one of the most complex and fascinating military aircraft, particularly its fully-automatic terrain-following radar system

(TFR). The important words there are fully-automatic, for the TFR guides the aircraft at a predetermined altitude by direct command to the appropriate channel of the aircraft's flight control system. An F-111 can thus offer a uniquely terrifying experience, precisely following *every* contour of the landscape at 200 feet and Mach .9 in total darkness or zero visibility while the crew sit with their arms crossed, skimming unseen mountains and valleys a quarter-second away from explosive oblivion, or in good light getting a very close-to geology lesson. Aardvark pilots call it 'skiing', and they can select the quality of ride given by the TFR: soft, where the aircraft makes gentle pull-ups over rising ground; medium, which is a little less comfortable; or hard, where the pull up is delayed until the aircraft is close to the hill, mountain or whatever and is

pulled up hard to a zero *g* pushover over the top. Most unnerving of all is that the F-111 makes these manoeuvres without any movement of the control column: *direct* command it is.

Close companion to the TRS is the WSO's (don't these acronyms get confusing?) Attack Radar System (ARS), a high-resolution, jam-resistant radar. The resolution is so good it can pick up telephone wires several miles from the airfield when the aircraft is parked. The WSO pre-sets his target co-ordinates before the flight, and as the TRS guides the F-111 in below enemy radar cover he can call up the target close in and a pair of cross-hairs on the ARS scope immediately lock on to its location while the Ballistics Computer Unit (BCU) automatically adjusts the weaponry for changes of heading, airspeed and altitude using information derived from the aircraft's Inertial Navigation System (yes, and it makes your jaw ache, doesn't it? — the INS) for pinpoint delivery of two nuclear bombs or up to 4,000 pounds of high explosive from the internal bomb bay and 3,000 pounds of ordnance from wing pylons. Not surprisingly the F-111's performance in Vietnam earned it yet another name: Whispering Death, coined by North Vietnamese forces who suffered its unheralded attacks. Me, I prefer yet another acronym. TFX: *Terrific Flying Experience,* or in the words of Secretary for Defence Robert S. McNamara who brought the world around his ears for ordering it in the first place, 'the greatest single step forward in combat aircraft in several decades'. When the Aardvark steps out, no-one hears it coming.

An FB-111 development aircraft with underwing stores. The inboard stores pylons swivel with wingsweep to keep stores aligned with airflow; the outer four pylons do not swivel and must be jettisoned before the aircraft can go supersonic, and are thus rarely used.

Learjet

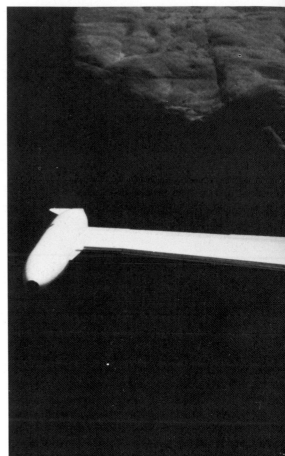

Truly it is the only way to go: soft hide furnishings and walnut veneer, muted lighting, Sinatra on the stereo, a glass of single malt whisky to sip as you cruise in shirtsleeve comfort nine miles above the surface, above all the bustling knee-to-chin airline travellers, up where the sky is beginning to turn blue-black and you can just make out the curvature of the earth as you barrel through empty skies at eight miles a minute.

In the late 1950s the idea of a private jet was revolutionary. Air travellers were only just seeing the first jet airliners in service, and although the Lockheed and North American companies were both proposing civilian versions of their Jet-Star and Sabreliner military transports, William P. Lear's proposal was something quite different: a low-cost personal jet which would sell for $400,000 and would carry just six passengers. It would be a reliable, simple aeroplane. 'My Jet,' Lear noted mischievously, 'will be a two-lever airplane: set lever A, then leave 'er be!'

Bill Lear was no naive newcomer to the aviation scene. Born in Mark Twain country in Hannibal, Missouri in 1902, Lear had set up in business at the age of 13 exploiting an inborn talent for electronics, and had made and lost fortunes with inventions ranging from car radios to aircraft automatic direction finders and high-speed executive transport conversions of wartime Lockheed Lodestar transports. His critics had often been proven wrong, but this time the long-suffering board of directors of Lear Incorporated would have none of it. *No private jets.* Ever contemptuous of the comfortable no-risks way of business, Lear sold his share of the company and took himself to Switzerland, where he set up the Swiss-American Aircraft Corporation. The Swiss move was no mere whim. Lear had his eye on the Pilatus P-16 ground-attack fighter which had been built there.

Although the basic aircraft was sound, it was plagued by inadequate systems and had no future as a military aircraft, but Lear saw within the fighter the basis for his private jet. He hired Dr Hans Studer, a former Dornier employee, and a respected American aircraft engineer named Gordon Israel, to mate the P-16's wings with a new fuselage. Ten million dollars of Lear's personal fortune went into the SAAC-23 prototype as bankers shied away from this seemingly doom-laden enterprise. Industry pundits forecast oblivion for the aircraft: it would fly too high, and no one would buy it. Lear persevered. Frustrated by the slow pace of development in sleepy Switzerland, he shipped the entire project back to Wichita, Kansas in 1962, and on 7 October 1963 the first Lear Jet (now Learjet) 23 made its maiden flight. Lear had such faith in his aeroplane that he tooled up for production even before the Lear Jet was certificated by American airworthiness authorities, but then Lear was always a make-or-break gambler, and this time the dice rolled in his favour. The Lear Jet was set to begin a dynasty. It was the first purpose-designed business jet, and has become the archetype of the breed. Its performance was a quantum leap from the tired, rebuilt, old warplanes

A fine head-on view of a Learjet 35A. Wingtip fuel tanks have been a feature of all Learjets except the latest 28/29 and 50-series models which have extended wings with upturned winglets at their tips.

which had been the mainstay of corporate aircraft fleets in the United States. A Lear Jet could fly at 540 mph at 41,000 feet and it could outclimb the early Century-series jet fighters in service with the United States Air Force. It was beautiful, downright *desirable* to look at. It had *style*. And although, as its critics pointed out, you could not stand up in its cabin ('Nor can you in your Cadillac,' countered Lear) it very quickly became a status symbol, from whose door people whom the newspapers called 'The Learjet Set'

would be delighted to be seen stepping.

Records fell to the Lear Jet, too. On 21 May 1965 a Lear made a dawn-to-dusk transcontinental flight from Los Angeles to New York City and back in 10 hours, 21 minutes; later that year another Lear Jet set a time-to-climb record, reaching 40,000 feet in seven minutes 21 seconds and thus proving its ability to get above the weather quickly; while in May 1966 a Lear Jet 24 with four people aboard circled the earth in 50 hours and 20 minutes flying time.

Early Lear Jet, the 23. This example was bought by Frank Sinatra.

Bill Lear, the very personification of the word dynamism, was not a man to enjoy — or even tolerate — standing still. While the factory churned out his jets to be sold haphazardly through a sketchy network of inexperienced dealers, he was engrossed in another project: an eight-track cartridge stereo player system for automobiles. The stereo business lost money, and by 1967 Lear Jet industries was looking shaky, despite a full order book, when Charles C. Gates, President of Gates Rubber Company of Denver, Colorado, bought out Bill Lear's 62 percent holding. The company was renamed Gates-Learjet Corporation, and the Lear Jet (Bill Lear had insisted on separating the words) became the Learjet. By this time a stretched 10-seat Learjet 25 was flying and had already knocked 58 seconds off the old time-to-40,000-feet record. 'They were building one hell of a product, but their system of selling it was ruining them,' explains Gates-Learjet's president Harry Combs. Slowly the new management began nursing the ailing company back to health, gradually refining the Learjet 24 and 25 models until, in 1973, the first new models for seven years were introduced. The Model 23, 24 and 25 Learjets were powered by pure-jet General Electric CJ-610 engines, excellent, reliable powerplants. But the coming of the 1970s brought an awareness of the need for fuel conservation and the need to take environmental considerations into account in aircraft operations, for pure-jet engines are by nature noisy beasts, and thirsty ones, too. The new Learjets 35 and 36 were powered by quieter, fuel-efficient Garrett AiResearch TFE-731 turbofan engines, which not only made Learjets more acceptable neighbours at environmentally-sensitive airports, but offered substantial increases in range. With four of its eight passenger seats filled, plus two crew, a Learjet 35A will fly 2,635 miles and still have a 45-minute fuel reserve; the comparable figures for the current pure-jet Learjet 25D with the same load is 1,647 miles. The six-passenger Learjet 36A does even better.

The introduction of the fanjet Lears assured Gates-Learjet of their annual position at the head of the business-jet manufacturing league. Production was soon running at seven aircraft per month, and by April 1975 the 500th Learjet had been delivered — 170 more than any other business jet. A year later Gates-Learjet pulled off a spectacular publicity coup when Arnold Palmer, himself a Learjet owner, flew a Model 36 around the world in a total flying time of 48 hours and

opposite
High and handsome. The fanjet-engined Learjet 36A cruises over England during a customer demonstration flight.

Flight deck of a Learjet 35A with weather radar screen mounted centrally above the power levers for its fuel-efficient Garrett AiResearch TFE-731 turbofan engines.

opposite
Latest Learjet model is this Learjet 55, which has a larger cabin than previous models providing 'stand up' headroom. The upturned surfaces at the wingtips are Whitcomb Winglets, which reduce drag and substantially improve the aircraft's cruise performance. Their appearance has earned the Learjet 55 the nickname 'Longhorn'.

48 minutes to celebrate the Bicentennial.

Staying ahead of the game was always Bill Lear's strongpoint — indeed he would usually invent the game — and Harry Combs has the same business philosophy. 'We never believe that we have the ultimate airplane,' he says of his company's continuing search for improvement, typified by the latest 'Longhorn' Learjet 55 and 56, which will begin customer deliveries in 1981. The 50-series Learjets are the most radical developments of Bill Lear's original design yet. A new fuselage incorporates a 10-passenger cabin with stand-up headroom (follow that, Cadillac) while the wingtip fuel-tanks which have always been a distinguishing feature of Learjets have given way to turned-up near-vertical, sail-like devices at the tips known as Whitcomb Winglets, hence the 'Longhorn' nickname. The winglets turn wingtip drag into useful lift, measurably increasing the aircraft's efficiency (and thus cruise performance and fuel economy) at high

altitude. And they can go high. The Longhorns and the Learjet 25D are approved for flight up to 51,000 feet, higher than any other civilian aircraft habitually flies save for Concorde. In general, the higher you fly in a jet, for any given weight and airspeed, the better your fuel consumption, and the faster you get up there the greater the saving. Learjets, always fighter-like in climb performance, can go arrow-straight to their maximum altitude; many other business jets must 'step-climb', levelling off at intervals to burn-off fuel and reduce weight before proceeding upward.

When the first Lear Jet 23s appeared it was part of the salesmen's technique to demonstrate to potential customers a maximum performance climb. Company pilots loved it, grinning behind the distinctive windshield that makes every Learjet look as if it is wearing a stylish pair of Italian wrap-round sunglasses, but I doubt that it did much for the chairman of the board sitting in the back trying not to spill his complimentary tumbler of scotch as the jet tilted back into a rocket climb. Subtle marketing was never Bill Lear's forte, and it is no surprise that many of his first customers were the kind of people who would arrive at the welcoming door of their Lear Jet not in a chauffeur-driven limousine but at the wheel of a Shelby Cobra. The Lear had the same *macho* appeal: radical looks, with a promise (more like a threat) of hair-tingling performance, sex, power and money in one neat package. Under Bill Lear's flamboyant direction the Lear Jet became a status-symbol aeroplane, the outward sign of a glossy-magazine life-style. Frank Sinatra had one. So too did Mr and Mrs Onassis. Whatever business jet the glittering stars arrived in, the society columns would call it a Lear Jet, which must have irritated the manu-facturers of rival aeroplanes. Under Gates-Learjet's guidance the emphasis has swung, rightly, to the aeroplane as a business tool.

Either way the Lear Jet/Learjet has achieved recognition beyond the con-fines of cocktail parties, airport ramps, pilot's lounges and company board-rooms. The second Model 23 hangs today in the National Air & Space Museum in Washington, D.C., and more than 1,000 other Learjets are flying around the world, the legacy of a brave and visionary gambler whose foresight ('too soon is just

right' was one of his favourite axioms) ushered in a new era of personal and business travel. Bill Lear died of leukemia on 14 May 1978, before he could see through his last project, a single-propeller, twin-turbine-engine business aircraft called Lear Fan which promises to start another revolution, for it has a struct-ure made up entirely of man-made compo-site materials, graphites and epoxies. They say it will never sell, it's short on . . .

above
Elegant decor is typical of the Learjet cabin.

Pitts Special

Curtis Pitts made a big splash in 1972. In the swimming pool of an hotel in Salon-de-Provence, France, whence he was flung, fully clothed, by jubilant members of the United States Aerobatic Team. It was their way of thanking him for making possible the first ever American team victory in the World Aerobatics Championships, the Olympic Games of competitive aerobatic flying: Pitts had designed the tiny biplanes in which they flipped and flopped their way to the prestigious Nesterov Trophy, named after the Imperial Russian Air Service pilot, Peter Nicholaivich Nesterov, who performed the first ever loop in 1913 (and was promptly banished to the guardhouse for his 'useless audacity'.)

The groundwork for the American victory began 30 years previously in 1942 when Curtis Pitts, then working for the U.S. Navy in Florida, had a notion to acquire an aeroplane which would perform aerobatic manoeuvres which his Waco UPF biplane would not. The only way was to design his own, so he did, combining the best elements of two classic aerobatic designs — the American Great Lakes and German Bücker Jungmeister. This was the first Pitts Special (the generic term has been applied to a number of aircraft of differing configuration, but for our purposes we are talking about aerobatic biplanes, not the midget racers and other types which 'Pa' Pitts called his 'Specials.') It performed remarkably well on a 55 hp Lycoming engine, but even better when Curtis installed a 90 hp Franklin and devised inverted fuel and oil systems for sustained inverted flight. Alas, the inverted systems worked either very well or not at all, and there was no telling which way it would be until you tried it. One day in 1945, after Pitts had sold the aeroplane to a nearly-deaf Florida cropduster, its new owner failed to notice the sudden silence after he had rolled the little biplane on its back at low level, and it was wrecked in the ensuing heavy landing. The pilot walked away, though, and Curtis began constructing a run of ten more Specials for a Gainesville, Florida company. Sadly the company also crashed, just after Pitts had completed the first aircraft. The Special, named *Li'l Stinker,* eventually found its way into the hands of a young lady named Betty Skelton, who was to captivate airshow watchers on both sides of the Atlantic in her diminutive red and white striped biplane. She performed at the *Daily Express* International Air Pageant at Gatwick Airport near London in 1949. 'The reaction to *Li'l Stinker* was astounding,' she recalled. 'I think it was about the smallest airplane flying at that time . . . they just fell in love with it.' Betty and her *Li'l Stinker,* with its black-and-white skunk emblem, won the US women's aerobatic title four times in a row between 1948 and 1951.

Curtis Pitts built a third Special named *Black Beauty* for another lady flier, Caro Bayley, but the 1950s were bleak times for acrobatics and for more than 10 years Curtis and his wife Willie Mae concentrated on running their cropdusting business in Gainesville, selling just the occasional set of plans for their tiny biplane to homebuilders.

In the 1960s came a revival of interest in serious competition aerobatics in the United States and the organization of the first formal world aerobatic competitions, using a scoring system devised by a Spanish count, José Aresti. Aresti evolved the *Sistema Aerocriptografica Aresti,* a kind of shorthand whereby every aerobatic manoeuvre (and there are something like 100,000 possible permutations) can be written down in graphic symbol form and whole sequences drawn up like a piece of music on a stave, with a 'K' or difficulty factor assigned to each.

A Pitts S-2S in knife-edge flight, with part of its lift coming from the fuselage side.

Over the top. The U.S. Red
Devils formation aerobatic
team pulling up into a loop in
their Pitts S-1S Specials.

below
Striped 'sunburst' paint jobs
are de rigueur for Pitts
Specials. This S-1S was flown
by American champion Bob
Herendeen at the 1970 World
Aerobatics Championships at
RAF Hullavington, England.

Aresti placed greatest emphasis (and highest potential scores) on manoeuvres in the vertical plane, when the aircraft is ascending or descending. At this time aerobatics was dominated by Eastern bloc nations, the Czechs, Poles and Hungarians in their Zlins and the Russians in their YAKs — all monoplanes — while the British, French, Spanish and Swiss struggled gamely with elderly biplanes. The Americans were simply not in the running, and the Pitts — regarded by many as a not-too-serious toy — seemed an unlikely challenger, because biplanes are at a natural disadvantage in vertical climbing manoeuvres, when the drag from wings, struts and bracing wires slows them down and great power is needed to keep the aeroplane climbing. (Conversely, when *descending* vertically the biplane's drag works in its favour, preventing an excessive speed build-up).

Curtis Pitts, who had once had ambitions of becoming world champion aerobatic pilot, was watching developments in Europe with interest. In 1962 he improved the basic Special design to accommodate engines of up to 180 hp. In 1965 he enlarged the open cockpit (allegedly to allow for his own spreading waistline), and a year later he made perhaps the most significant change, developing a set of symmetrical airfoil-section wings with four ailerons to improve the aeroplane's inverted capability and roll rate. Pitts used two different airfoil sections for the upper and lower wings and patented his design: these 'competition' wings were available only as custom-built sets made by Pitts

himself, and then only to selected customers. One such was airline pilot Bob Herendeen, who came to Europe for his first World Championship at Moscow in 1966, placing 25th. He came third at Magdeburg in 1968, then burst onto the scene spectacularly at RAF Hullavington in England in 1970, flying a finely-tuned 180 hp competition Pitts S-1S which was a breathtaking education to watch. Though a Russian won the contest, the Pitts Specials flown by four members of the American team won the hearts of spectators. They seemed absurdly small, spanning just 17 feet, but their climb rate, roll rate (180 degrees per second) and ability to perform mind-boggling snap manoeuvres one after another were simply breathtaking — cheeky and snappy compared to the graceful YAKs, which one observer described as 'grand piano aeroplanes'. If so, the Pittses were like xylophones. 'Good aeroplanes for fun. No good for contests,' a Russian pilot opined after flying a Pitts. He placed eighteenth. Bob Herendeen came second.

Two years later at Salon-de-Provence the American team, now all flying Pitts Specials, made a clean sweep, winning the team and individual men's and women's trophies, and Pa Pitts got his ducking in the pool for a lifetime's ambition realized, albeit as a designer and builder rather than as a pilot.

Unlike the S-1 Special, which was never intended as an off-the-shelf aeroplane, but rather as a home-built or custom-built craft, the two-seat S-2A introduced in 1971 (though it first flew, named, inevitably, *Big Stinker*, in 1966) was designed from the outset for factory production. Curtis Pitts had endless trouble getting the US Federal Aviation Administration to certificate it for production, for airworthiness authorities are universally a conservative bunch who look with suspicion on aerobatic machines, at least when they have to rubber-stamp the paperwork. After years of wrangling the FAA finally quibbled over some trifling detail in the tailwheel design, so Pitts fired off a long technical report carefully composed so that the first letters of the paragraphs spelled out some very rude words indeed. Whether the FAA ever caught on I do not know, but they did grant the S-2A a type certificate, and the aeroplane immediately became the first choice of aerobatic flight schools and formation aerobatics teams the world over, notably with the Rothmans Team in England, the Carling Red Tops in Canada, and the Royal Jordanian Falcons in Jordan. The two seater S-2A is slightly larger all round than the S-1, with a 200 hp Lycoming engine driving a constant-speed propeller. A 260 hp S-2S competition single-seater based on the larger airframe is also available from the Pitts factory in Wyoming, though Curtis Pitts has sold out his interest and now enjoys retirement, taking a royalty on every aircraft sold.

Although newer designs more suited to the ever changing demands of top-class competition aerobatics have emerged, the Pitts remains the dream machine for an aspiring aerobatic pilot, the choice of champions. More than 3,000 sets of plans have been sold to homebuilders and several hundred are flying.

Why so successful? Essentially because the Pitts has evolved over a protracted gestation period into a near-perfect flying machine for the pilot who wants to spend as little time as possible right side up. The airframe is immensely strong, stressed for +9g and —4½g — almost impossible to break, indeed to the best of my knowledge no Pitts built the way Curtis intended has ever come unglued in the air, though the fatiguing

Smoke on, go. A Pitts S-2A of the British Rothmans Aerobatic Team blowing smoke and knife-edging for the author's camera. Note that the pilot is holding plenty of right rudder to keep the Pitts' nose raised in knife-edge flight.

'Old Glory' reproduced on the wings and tail of a Pitts S-1S photographed at the Experimental Aircraft Association's annual fly-in at Oshkosh, Wisconsin.

effect of constant aerobatics means that the steel-tubing which makes up the fuselage frame needs to be inspected regularly. With a 180 hp engine and a gross weight of just 1,140 lbs the Pitts S-1S has a better than excellent power/weight ratio for vertical manoeuvres. One specially-modified Pitts in the United States has a nitrous-oxide boosted engine giving 340 hp. It climbs like a Saturn V rocket and can perform multiple vertical rolls, eight- and sixteen-point vertical rolls and long, long prop-hangs. The short-span wings and four ailerons provide for very high rates of roll around 180 degrees per second, while the highly-stressed air-frame permits snap rolls (which are in essence horizontal spins) to be entered at high airspeeds producing rotation rates up to 260 degrees per second, so fast that your stomach is back straight and level before your head knows it has been away. Climb rate, either way up thanks to Curtis Pitts' symmetrical-section wings, is in the order of 2,600 feet per minute after a take-off which is too quick to be troublesome, typically around four seconds of ground roll.

The Pitts' most endearing quality is its control response and harmony. The torque-tube and ball-bearing operated ailerons

are feather-light, with no friction. On my first ever ride in a brand-new Pitts S-2A with the late Manx Kelly, founder of the Rothmans Aerobatic Team, I was handed the stick to try for myself. Accustomed to the soggy unresponsive trainers which I had flown I thought a moderate-rate turn would not tax my abilities too much, and proceeded to push the stick firmly to the left side of the cockpit. I think we were about half way through our *second* aileron roll when Manx caught it and rolled us back level. Luckily there was no intercom so I was spared the oaths that were whipped away in the slipstream.

Provided that you know what control movements are required for any given manoeuvre a Pitts will respond to the mere thought, so that returning to lesser machines after flying a Pitts is likely to deflate the ego of a would-be aerobatic ace. Curtis Pitts cautions homebuilders against over-confidence in their machines, which can easily flatter a not especially competent aerobatic pilot into foolishness. A Pitts moves around the sky very quickly and will get through an aerobatic sequence at a greater pace than other aircraft, so it is vital to keep ahead of the aeroplane mentally. In skilled hands a Pitts, especially the 180-200 hp single-seaters, will perform any manoeuvre that you can call to mind, and a few that you might rather not. If it has faults, they are forgiven for the sheer elation of its performance. True, the forward visibility on the ground or in the circuit for landing is terrible, in either single or two-seater. And perhaps the aeroplane is too small to be seen properly from the ground when performing sequences at the heights used in international competition aerobatics, but I challenge you to find any red-blooded pilot whose eyes don't just glaze over a little at the sight of a sunburst-striped Pitts, or one who would not leap at the offer of a flight in one.

Even Curtis Pitts himself, who fettled his design to perfection over a quarter century, says this of the Special: 'There were lots of times when I felt pretty good, but I would say that the first time I flew the first little airplane was the biggest thrill for me. It was like a ride in a skyrocket after flying those other airplanes.' Exactly. A Pitts Special is *very* special.

Pitts Special cockpit. Note the card with pilot Philip Meeson's aerobatic competition sequence of manoeuvres annotated in the 'shorthand' developed by Spanish pilot José Aresti.

Colourfully bedecked Pitts S-1S flown by U.S. lady aerobatic champion Mary Gaffaney.

175

Boeing 747

Consider a few statistics. Between four and five million components go into its construction. The parts are supplied by 1,500 contractors and 15,000 supplementary suppliers in 49 States of the Union and dozens of foreign countries. The assembly plant, which stands where once was a 100-acre forest, has 285 million cubic feet of space. It is the world's biggest building, so immense that inspection staff *drive* from one end of the assembly line to the other. One hundred and twenty-five miles of wiring are needed to bring life-blood to the aeroplane's electrical systems. And it costs about $50 million a copy, give or take a few million.

It is difficult not to get carried away with such golly-gosh trivia when talking about the Boeing 747, first of the so-called 'jumbo' jets and still the world's largest commercial airliner. First news of this mammoth was broken on 13 April 1966, when Boeing announced that Pan American Airways had placed a $525 million order for 25 new jet airliners capable of seating between 350 and 500 passengers. Boeing had already investigated the special problems associated with very large aircraft with a bid for the United States Air Force's CX contract, eventually awarded to the Lockheed C-5A Galaxy, but a commercial aircraft was an entirely different proposition. Though weighing twice as much, and carrying up to three times as many passengers, the 747 would need to be able to operate from existing airport runways used by the Boeing 707. And there was the problem not just of accommodating 500 souls, but of getting them on and off quickly.

Boeing opted for a single-deck cabin divided into four sections with two aisles, seating nine or ten passengers in each 20-foot row in blocks of three-four-two/three. A 16-seat first class section, 32-seat economy class section, or a cocktail lounge could be accommodated on an upper deck reached via a novel spiral staircase. Each section had its own movie screen, and ten passenger doors were provided, though in practice no more than three are used routinely. Great care was taken in interior styling to provide an aura of spaciousness more akin to an ocean liner than a jet, far removed from the claustrophobic oppressiveness of earlier narrow-body airliners.

The first Boeing 747 — a production standard aircraft; there was no prototype — flew on 9 February 1969. Amazingly for such an innovative and complex new aeroplane, the first passenger service with the 747 was operated by Pan American less than a year later, on 22 January 1970, from New York to London.

Boeing selected Pratt & Whitney JT9D-3D turbofan engines for the 747, each of which provided 43,500 pounds of thrust, enabling the aircraft to operate comfortably from any runway which could handle a Boeing 707. Variants of the 747 are now offered with a choice of up-rated JT9Ds, General Electric CF6s, or Rolls-Royce RB-211s, of up to 53,000 pounds thrust apiece.

Equally vital to the aircraft's airfield performance is the wing design, which combines very high sweepback (on a commercial airliner) of thirty-seven degrees for efficient high-speed cruise with an array of leading and trailing edge high-lift devices to enhance low-speed handling, so that a 747 will actually get off the ground in a shorter distance than a proportionately-loaded 707. Each wing panel has 13 fibreglass leading-edge slats, the outer ten changing shape from flat to curved as they move outboard to increase wing camber and stabilize airflow during low airspeed/high angle of attack flight, while triple-slotted trailing edge flaps extending to the outboard engine pylons provide a total wing area increase of 21 percent and an increased lift component

of some 90 percent, bringing the aircraft's stalling speed in landing configuration down to remarkably low figures of about 110 knots (the precise stalling speed is determined by aircraft weight) or below. The efficiency of all this slottery and flappery may be gauged from the knowledge that with the wing 'clean' stall speed increases by more than 50 percent. All of which makes the 747 as easy to fly as any of its smaller contemporaries, indeed easier than most.

If you have flown in the passenger cabin of a 747 you will have some impression of its sheer size, and you may have concluded that the flight deck crew enjoy similar spaciousness. Not so. Paradoxically the Jumbo's cockpit, perched high up on the second deck (if you sit in the fourth row, left hand side of the forward first class section, the captain's size-10s will be right above your head) is just as tight a squeeze as those of the smaller airline jets. What distinguishes the 747's flight deck is its unique viewpoint, 30 feet above the ground. From this lofty perch, people, other aeroplanes and taxiways seem absurdly small. Imagine a building some 75 yards long and 70 yards wide, put yourself at a third-floor window with no sight of the building's peripheral extremities, contemplate the whole thing

The first 747, Old No. 1, pictured here with an earlier Boeing product, a Model 100 biplane restored by the company's chief test pilot Lew Wallick as a U.S. Army P.12 pursuit ship.

moving at your command, and you have a fair idea of how the newcomer to the Jumbo Jet feels the first time he tries to taxy it. At least at smaller airports the elevated flight deck gives you a chance to cast disdainful looks *down* at tower controllers. Steering on the ground is controlled with a small hand-tiller. The temptation to forget that there is more than 200 feet of aeroplane behind the cockpit and steer along taxiway lines with the nosewheel must be resisted; the main landing gear is about 90 feet behind the flight deck and unless the nose of the

aircraft is allowed to overshoot each turn by a wide margin, before bringing the rest of the aeroplane around, there is every likelihood that the 16-wheel main undercarriage bogies will cut the corner and leave 350 tons of aeroplane embarrassingly stranded in the rough.

The high viewpoint can be misleading on speeds, too. What seems to be a snail's pace crawl along a taxiway may actually appear on the groundspeed readout of the Inertial Navigation System (INS) as a good clip of 35 knots or more. Even at take-off power the lack of noise from the

Jumbo's flight deck gives few clues to the overall size of the aircraft.

quiet, high bypass ratio turbofans and the apparent remoteness of the runway give an impression of sluggish acceleration and a take-off roll which threatens to go on forever (and actually lasts some 40-45 seconds at typical operational weights) before the first officer calls 'V1' (the speed at which the aircraft is committed to the take-off), then 'Rotate' and the captain eases back on the control column to raise the nose ten degrees initially, then further back to raise it about fifteen degrees (the two-segment rotation is used to avoid the possibility of the aircraft's rear fuselage bumping the runway) for lift-off, by which time the 747 will have consumed a mile and a half of runway and accelerated to nearly 200 mph. Even at that not inconsiderable speed something tells you that an aeroplane this big, this heavy, simply cannot fly, an anxious moment of doubt, before the landing gear comes up and the 747 starts to thrust forward, when all 350 tons of it seem just to hang there, motionless. You will see more white knuckles in the passenger cabins at that instant than at any other time on the flight.

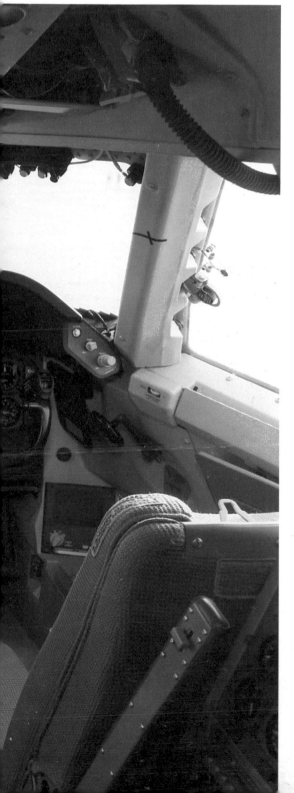

'She's a sweet-handling old lady, as easy to fly, I think, as a Tiger Moth,' says a 747 captain friend of mine. In routine airline service, crossing continents and oceans at six miles high, there is actually little hand-flying of the aeroplane to be done. The autopilot takes care of flying the aeroplane, the INS looks after navigation, steering to pre-programmed 'waypoints' along the route with uncanny accuracy, within yards rather than miles, and the four turbofans burn fuel at the rate of fifteen tons an hour while pushing the aeroplane along at 500 knots at economy cruise power settings. But even under manual control the 747 provides few reminders that you are towing several hundred tons of aeroplane behind you. Pitch and roll controls are very light and responsive, and the rudder forces are such that the asymmetric loads created by the failure of an outboard engine can easily be contained with the rudder pedals by the pilot, with little chance of his leg going into muscular spasm before he can trim off the pressure. *Immaculate* is the word most frequently used to describe the 747's handling qualities.

Boeing 747 climbing away at dusk.

The 747 was the first American airliner to be fully equipped for automatic landing (the British Hawker Siddeley Trident has been approved for auto-landing since 1966). In autoland mode a second autopilot comes into play when the radio altimeter gives a height readout of 1,500 feet and tracks the Instrument Landing System which provides directional and vertical guidance to the runway. Automatic throttle control maintains whatever power is necessary to keep the aircraft at pre-selected airspeeds as the aircraft's configuration changes (when landing gear and flaps are lowered for example, calling for large increases in power to counteract the additional drag) right down to 60 feet above the runway when the throttles are closed smoothly and the aircraft rotated into the landing attitude ready for the massive spring-loaded undercarriage bogies to cushion the shock of touchdown. The sensitive radio altimeter is corrected, incidentally, to take into account the 747's height above ground, something which calls for practice when landing manually for there are no visual cues and the high-set flight deck seems still to be 'flying' way above the runway when the wheels are already brushing the tarmac.

So familiar is the Jumbo at airports the world over that it is all too easy to become blasé about the aeroplane. And that is to do it an injustice. The Boeing 747 has possibly had a greater effect on air travel than any other aeroplane in history, including the DC-3. The 747 is not just another very large aeroplane. When it first appeared all previous thinking about airliner and airport capacities had to be doubled at a stroke. Here was not just a new aeroplane but a whole new order in mass travel which has opened up opportunities for cheap air journeys and made intercontinental travel a reality for people (it has been estimated that four million passengers travel on 747s every month) who have never previously purchased an airline ticket. Not only passenger travel has been revolutionized by the Jumbo. Its corpulent airframe is readily adaptable to freight-carrying, in all-cargo (in case you have not had your fill of statistics, someone has calculated that you can get 200 Volkswagen Beetles or two tennis courts into a 747's cargo hold) or mixed passenger/cargo roles. And there are projected stretched 747s which will be able to carry more than 700 passengers. One last statistic? The present record for squeezing passengers into a Jumbo — a sport which seems to have taken over from cramming students into telephone booths — stands at 674 people, and was set by a Quantas Jumbo evacuating hurricane victims from the city of Darwin.

Other airlines are now adopting American Airline's natural metal finish, seen here on a 747. Lack of overall paintwork saves weight and leads to greater fuel economy.

opposite
The 747 assembly plant at Everett, Washington, is the world's largest building by volume, with 285 million cubic feet of space.

181

Concorde

Breakfast in London, lunch in New York, dinner in Paris. Time-travel for the price (albeit a very high price) of an airline ticket.

If you dine instead at one of the hotel restaurants which border London's Heathrow Airport your meal may be interrupted by an outburst of applause from your fellow diners. This is no gesture of appreciation for some culinary masterpiece, but a spontaneous display of approval for the aeroplane which has just landed on the adjacent runway — Concorde, whose elegantly sculptured airframe embodies one of man's most outstanding technical triumphs, or one of his most extravagant follies, depending on your point of view.

You know about Concorde, of course? No? Let us then travel back through time, to the early 1950s when aviation fuel was cheap and speed rather than economy

was the keynote of air travel. Newspapers were full of stories about military jets 'breaking the sound barrier', likening transonic flight to a circus animal bursting through a paper hoop. But if jet fighters could do it, why not a faster-than-sound airliner? The Royal Aircraft Establishment at Farnborough, England, always at the forefront of supersonic research (and always seeking to justify its very existence in the face of ill-founded public criticism), pondered the matter. If in doubt, form a committee. They did, and this august body duly recommended that not one but *two* supersonic transports were needed: a 100-seat medium range machine to cruise at Mach 1.2 (800 mph), and a 150-seat Transatlantic aeroplane which would cruise at Mach 1.8 (1,200 mph). After much official deliberation a government contract was eventually awarded to the Bristol Aero-

plane Company (later British Aircraft Corporation, now swallowed up in the British Aerospace conglomerate) for a design study for a 100-passenger aircraft with Trans-atlantic range. The French, meanwhile, were also toying with a supersonic airliner — the medium range Sud Aviation Super Caravelle. An uneasy marriage of the two ideas was sealed with an agreement in November 1962 whereby the British and French Governments would underwrite the development costs (and share the profits) on a 50/50 basis, and production aircraft would be assembled in both countries. British enthusiasm for the deal, which had no escape clause, was fired by the belief that it would ease Britain's entry into the European Economic Community. Alas, it did not. And in his famous 'Non' speech a few months later President Charles de Gaulle did little to soften the blow by announcing that the joint SST project would henceforth be called Concorde, with an 'e'. *Our* aeroplane, retorted Britain in a fit of chauvinism, will be called Concord, without an 'e'. This absurd dual spelling, symptomatic of the less than cordial entente which attended the aircraft's creation, persisted until the day the (French) prototype Concorde 001 was rolled out of its hangar at Toulouse in December 1967. Mistake me not, the concord which existed between BAC (British Aerospace) and Sud Aviation (Aerospatiale) during the gestation period was a model of international co-operation, but at government level there is little doubt that escalating costs running riot would have caused Britain to pull out had anyone been monitoring the true cost of the aeroplane, or if there had been any way of bowing out without incurring even greater financial penalties.

The French prototype made its first flight from Toulouse on 2 March 1969, the British prototype, 002, from Filton, Bristol on 9 April, and the production aircraft flew their first commercial services on 21 January 1976, an Air France Concorde leaving Paris for Dakar and Rio de Janeiro at the same instant as a British Airways aircraft departed from London for Bahrein.

In the eighteen years between the signing of the joint-development agreement and Concorde's entry into service many things had changed: not least the development costs, confidently predicted at £150-170 million, which had risen to an incredible £2,000 million, and the expected sales of up to 500 aircraft to eager customers, which dwindled to just 16 aircraft — and those to the captive-market

The ogival delta wing shape and partially-lowered visor are visible in this low-speed cruise shot of one of British Airways' Concorde fleet.

national flag-carriers whose governments obligingly wrote off the aircraft's monumental acquisition costs. Commercially, Concorde has been an unmitigated disaster, failing to sell, and — largely because of its fuel-guzzling characteristics — unable to operate profitably.

But what of the technical achievement? Government mismanagement aside, the reason why the Concorde cost so much to develop is simply that BAC and Aerospatiale were treading virgin ground. Supersonic aircraft were not new, but a supersonic airliner is a very different machine to a military fighter. Military jets fly supersonic only in short bursts; the Concorde needed to be able to cruise supersonically for more than three hours, and it needed to be able to carry more than 100 passengers, which immediately raises the tricky problem of drag at high airspeed. The faster an aeroplane goes the more drag it creates. To counteract the drag while maintaining airspeed you need bigger engines, which burn more fuel so larger fuel tanks are needed, which means a bigger airframe, which creates even more drag, and on and on in a vicious self-defeating spiral. Inevitably the design had to be a compromise between speed, range and payload, and Concorde is. At a time when the wide-body airliners such as the Boeing 747 were doubling the number of passengers carried in a single aircraft, Concorde halved the figure (and the time needed to get there, of course). Its narrow cabin can

accommodate a maximum of 144 passengers in high density layout, but typically is configured for 128, with a further payload penalty in hot or high conditions. Range is sufficient for London-New York with enough fuel for a diversion to an alternate airport and standard holding reserves, no more. Speed? A maximum of Mach 2.2 (1,680 mph). Some military aircraft are capable of speeds in excess of Mach 3, why not Concorde? Because sharp rises in skin temperatures above Mach 2 would have required an airframe manufactured from expensive steels and titanium; Concorde, cruising just below the 'heat barrier', is constructed from aluminium alloy which can absorb the more modest temperature ranges (from —35 to +120 degrees Centigrade) to which it is subjected, without damage.

There were other problems besides questions of performance, range and payload. Although it was a revolutionary airliner quite unlike any previous commercial aircraft, Concorde had to operate from existing airports, be flown by ordinary pilots, not specially trained astronauts, and it had to provide passengers with a familiar, reassuring environment. The ogival delta wing incorporates subtle changes of camber, droop and twist in its airfoil surface to enhance the aircraft's handling at low speed. Delta wings are excellent for supersonic flight, but at low speeds they suffer penalties of high drag at high

Tiny cabin windows are evident in this ground view of Concorde, with 'droop-snoot' nose in raised position but with the protective visor lowered.

angles of attack, though the wing cannot stall in the conventional sense unless provoked into angles of attack outside the aircraft's normal operation. And there was the question of power. The 38,050-pounds thrust Olympus 593 engine developed for Concorde by Rolls-Royce and SNECMA was the major problem, not least because a variable geometry air intake had to be devised for it. Jet engines work most efficiently when intake air reaches the face of the engine at about half the speed of sound, so Concorde engineers had to find a way of decelerating the ram-air by some 1,000 mph within the length of the air intake — about 11 feet.

Certainly no commercial aircraft in history has ever incorporated so many innovations as Concorde, and not surprisingly it entered service as the most thoroughly tested airliner ever, with three times as many testing hours flown as the Boeing 747. Indeed the testing goes on, for a full-size airframe is, as I write, being subjected to day-in, day-out fatigue testing at RAE Farnborough,

Concorde flight deck is best described as 'cosy'. Note 'ram's horn' control columns and flight engineers station at right.

Concorde cruises above the tropopause, typically around 11 miles high, where no other commercial aircraft can operate.

clocking up 'flying' hours at three times the rate of the operational aircraft to determine the Concorde's structural life.

And day-in, day-out, Concorde continues to dash across the Atlantic, though the planned network of worldwide routes has failed to materialize, partly because of environmental objections which prevent the aircraft operating supersonically over land, thus defeating its object, but more importantly because the ever-rising cost of aviation fuel and the economies offered by wide-body fuel-efficient airliners such as the 747, DC-10 and TriStar have made it too expensive to operate.

Economy has taken its toll since the heady euphoric days of the first commercial Concorde operations. Gone are the gifts and trinkets which once were showered on the supersonic elite, the courtesy limousine rides into town, the unlimited free international telephone calls. You still get your own Concorde check-in and departure lounge though, so there is still opportunity to lord it over lesser mortals, and Concorde's tastefully-decorated coffee-and-cream cabin is hardly austere, though it is narrower and has smaller windows than even the early jetliners. Apart from that, and a digital machometer readout on the forward bulkhead, there is little to distinguish it.

The flight deck is even more cramped than is normal on airliners. Concorde operates with a crew of three: captain,

first-officer (co-pilot) and flight engineer. Their cockpit preparations begin one hour before scheduled departure time, by which time weather reports will have been gathered (Concorde flies so fast that up-to-date weather reports are vital — no use knowing what was happening four hours ago), a 'tactical chart' prepared which shows the aircraft's capability to continue the flight or return after a single or double engine failure at various predetermined points along its track, and fuel uplift agreed and entered onto a computer which calculates the aircraft's centre of gravity position. The C of G must be shifted in flight because as the aircraft accelerates the wing's centre of lift moves rearwards, and the C of G must be adjusted accordingly by transferring fuel. Concorde has 13 fuel tanks of which the two forward tanks set in the leading edges of the forward wing section are 'trim tanks' to which part of the 28,000-gallon fuel load can be pumped (or pumped out) to trim the aircraft. Lateral trim can be achieved by wing-to-wing fuel transfer. Conventional trimming by aerodynamic surfaces would cause too much drag in supersonic flight.

For taxying, take-off and landing the nose section of the aircraft droops — 12½ degrees on the ground and in approach configuration, five degrees for take-off and early stages of supersonic climb. A visor protects the cockpit windows

against kinetic heating at high speed cruise. A long taxi at high weight is bad news for Concorde, for its carbon-fibre brakes are liable to heat up to a point where the ability to stop the aircraft during an aborted take-off might be impaired.

Once cleared to roll, power is brought up to full afterburner on the four Olympus engines (Concorde is the only airliner with afterburning) — thrust equivalent to the combined output of 10,000 British Leyland Minis, or sufficient to heat and light a medium-sized town — and the aircraft rotated (for typical weights and ambient temperatures) at about 195-200 knots after a ground roll of some 40 seconds. The rotation angle is steep, so the crew lose sight of the ground. Initial lift-off angle, known as Theta 2, is maintained to ± ½ degree until the aircraft is rotated further to keep its speed down to 250 knots (maximum permissible in airport terminal control areas), at which point the deck angle is 18 degrees, and total fuel consumption with afterburner in the order of 14,000 gallons per hour. Afterburner comes off for noise abatement climb, accompanied by a pitch down to maintain 250 knots, and Concorde begins a subsonic climb to 28,000 feet over the Bristol Channel, where it starts accelerating through the transonic zone. Full afterburner is denoted by a noticeable nudge in the back as the added thrust comes on, but going supersonic is something of a non-event, its passage marked only by the Machmeter displaying the magic figure 1.00 and (usually) a round of applause from the passenger cabin. Standard procedure is to use afterburner to accelerate to Mach 1.7 then 'coast' on up in a cruise-climb to Mach 2. In fact Concorde never really levels off in the cruise, because its optimum speed depends on aircraft weight, which is constantly reducing as fuel burns off, and temperature, but a typical maximum altitude is 57,000 feet — 11 miles high and totally alone, for no other commercial aircraft is certificated to such lofty levels — with a maximum operating altitude of 60,000 feet. Total temperature must also be watched, monitored on a gauge which measures a combination of ambient and kinetic temperatures. Concorde's skin is limited to a maximum allowable temperature of 127 degrees Centigrade. Prolonged exposure to higher temperatures can adversely effect the aircraft's airframe life.

When deceleration point is reached the Olympuses are throttled back but the aircraft is held in the three-degrees nose up attitude of supersonic cruise until the speed bleeds off to Mach 1.6, when the descent is slowed to cross the North American coastline subsonically at 39,000 feet, maintaining 350 knots, then 250 knots in the airport Terminal Manoeuvring Area, nose drooped five degrees, visor down (there is a great increase in flight deck noise with visor lowered), with final approach flown between 155-180 knots in a markedly nose-high attitude of 11 degrees to 100 feet when the first officer calls radio altimeter heights continuously because the high angle of attack makes it difficult to judge visually. At fifteen feet the throttles are closed and the aircraft flared for touchdown. The delta wing builds up a cushion of air close to the ground which would actually put the aeroplane onto the ground without flaring it, but the arrival would likely be what one pilot euphemistically describes as 'a trifle over-firm'.

Concorde: success or failure? Commercially the aircraft has been a calamity, and, like the R-101 airship, a fine example of what happens when political and national prestige are allowed to hold sway over sound business sense. But as a technological achievement there is no denying that Concorde *is* a triumph, providing the well-heeled traveller with a supersonic leap forward which will surely not be topped until (and if) passenger space travel becomes commonplace.

PICTURE ACKNOWLEDGEMENTS

American Airlines 181. Les Anderson via Aviation Photos International 123 (top). Air Portraits 14-15, 19, 22-3, 24 (bottom), 43, 89, 94, 142-3, 166. Beech Aircraft Corp. 56, 60, 61, 129, 130, 132, 133. Boeing 113, 115 (bottom), 177, 178, 180. British Aerospace 42, 46 (bottom), 92, 93, 95, 97, 152, 153, 154, 156, 157, 182, 185. British Airways 63 (bottom), 64 (top and bottom), 66 (bottom), 79 (bottom), 138, 139, 184, 186. Austin J. Brown 135. Cessna Aircraft Company 148, 149, 150. Gates Learjet 165, 168, 169. General Dynamics 158-9, 160, 161, 162, 163. James Gilbert 12, 18, 32, 33, 77. Philip Jarrett 20, 21, 115 (top). Mike Jerram 16, 17, 24 (top), 26, 29, 30 (top), 31, 34-5, 37, 38-9, 40, 41, 44-5, 46 (top), 47, 48, 49, 57, 58-9, 63 (top), 66 (top), 68, 69, 70-71, 72, 73, 78, 79 (top), 81, 82 (top), 86-7, 88, 91, 96, 98, 99, 102, 107, 109 (top), 110-11, 118, 140, 146-7, 151, 155, 170-71, 172, 173, 174, 175, 179. Lockheed 104, 105, 108, 109 (bottom). McDonnell Douglas 144. Messer- schmitt-Bölkow-Blohm 82 (bottom), 83, 84, 85. Cole Palen 28. Stephen Piercey 74-5. Rockwell International 100, 101, 103, 116, 117, 119, 120, 121. Wim Schoenmaker 123 (bottom), 124, 125, 126. Shorts 64 (middle). Smithsonian Institut- ion 11 (both), 13. Time-Life Inc. 30 (bottom). United Airlines 76. U.S.A.F. 112. U.S. Navy 141, 145. Vickers Ltd. 90, 136-7.

SELECTED FURTHER READING

Ball, Larry. *Those Incomparable Bonanzas.* McCormick-Armstrong Co., Wichita, Kansas, 1971.

Boughton, Terence. *The Story of the British Light Aeroplane.* John Murray, London, 1963.

Bowyer, Chaz. *Sopwith Camel — King of Combat.* Glasney Press, Falmouth, 1978.

Bramson, Alan, and Birch, Neville. *The Tiger Moth Story.* Cassell, London, 1964.

Bryden, H.G. (Ed.). *Wings — An Anthology of Flight.* Faber & Faber, London, 1942.

Christy, Joe. *The Learjet.* TAB Books, Blue Ridge, Pa., 1979.

Combs, Harry. *Kill Devil Hill.* Houghton-Mifflin, Boston, Mass., 1979.

Davis, Larry. *MiG Alley.* Squadron/Signal Publications, Warren, Michigan, 1978.

De Havilland, Sir Geoffrey. *Sky Fever.* Hamish Hamilton, London, 1961.

Ford Motor Co. *1929 Ford Tri-Motor Manual,* Facsimile, Aviation Publications, Milwaukee, Wisconsin.

Francis, Devon. *Mr. Piper & His Cubs.* Iowa State University Press, Ames, Iowa, 1973.

Gallico, Paul. *The Hurricane Story.* Michael Joseph, London, 1969.

Gann, Ernest K. *Fate is the Hunter.* Hodder & Stoughton, London, 1961.

Gunston, Bill. *F-111.* Ian Allan, Shepperton, Middlesex, 1978.

Gruenhagen, Robert. *Mustang.* Arco, New York, 1969.

Gurney, Gene. *P-38 Lightning.* Arco, New York, 1969.

Hadingham, Evan. *The Fighting Triplanes.* Hamish Hamilton, London, 1968.

Higham, Robin, and Siddall, Abigail. *Flying Aircraft of the USAAF/USAF.* Iowa State University Press, Ames, Iowa, 1975.

Ingells, Douglas J. *The Plane That Changed the World.* Aero Books, Fallbrook, Cal., 1966. and *Tin Goose.* Aero Books, Fallbrook, Cal., 1968.

Jablonski, Edward. *Flying Fortress.* Doubleday, New York, 1965.

Knöke, Hans. *I Flew for the Führer.* Evans, London, 1965.

Lewis, Cecil. *Sagittarius Rising.* Peter Davis, London, 1936.

Ogilvy, David (Ed.). *From Blériot to Spitfire.* Airlife Publications, Shrewsbury, 1977.

Prest, Robert. *F-4 Phantom — A Pilot's Story.* Cassell, London, 1979.

Reynolds, Quentin. *They Fought For the Sky.* Cassell, London, 1958.

Smith, Robert T., and Lempicke, Thomas A. *Staggerwing!* Cody Publications, Kissimmee, Fla., 1979.

Stewart, Oliver. *Words and Music for a Mechanical Man.* Faber & Faber, London, 1967.

Stiles, Bert. *Serenade to the Big Bird.* Lindsay, Drummond, London, 1947.

Tallman, Frank. *Flying the Old Planes.* Doubleday, New York, 1973.

Toliver, Raymond, and Constable, Trevor. *Fighter Aces of the USA.* Aero Publishers, Fallbrook, California, 1979.

Van Ishoven, Armand. *Messerschmitt.* Gentry Books. London, 1975.